Building Services Integration

Building Services Integration

Paul K. Barton

Principle Lecturer in Construction Management,
Sheffield Polytechnic

formerly Senior Lecturer in Construction Management,
Leeds Polytechnic

with contributions by

Barry G. Fryer
Senior Lecturer in Construction Management
Leeds Polytechnic

David Highfield
Senior Lecturer in Construction Technology
Leeds Polytechnic

LONDON   NEW YORK
E. & F. N. SPON

First published 1983 by
E. & F. N. Spon Ltd
11 New Fetter Lane, London EC4P 4EE
Published in the USA by
E. & F. N. Spon
733 Third Avenue, New York NY10017

© *1983 Paul Barton*

Phototypeset by Sunrise Setting, Torquay
Printed in Great Britain
by J.W. Arrowsmith Ltd., Bristol

ISBN 0 419 12030 0

British Library Cataloguing in Publication Data

Barton, Paul K.
   Building services integration.

   Bibliography: p.
   Includes index.
   1. Building.   2. Construction industry–
Management.
   I. Fryer, Barry G. II. Highfield, David. III. Title.
   TH153.B365 1983   690'.068   83–334
   ISBN 0-419-12030-0

Library of Congress Cataloging in Publication Data

Barton, Paul, K.
   Building services integration.
   1. Buildings–Environmental engineering.
   I. Title   II. Fryer, Barry G.
   III. Highfield, David
   696   TH6021

   ISBN 0-419-12030-0

To Julie,
David, Naomi,
Michael and Peter

with love

Contents

Building Services Integration

Preface

In the 18th century a Client requiring a building would approach a Master Builder who was willing to undertake all the work involved from the initial design to the final decoration; as a result communication within the building process was relatively simple.

Since then, however, the situation has changed. The volume and complexity of building work has increased rapidly. Society has placed more constraints, not only in the form of legislation specifying minimum standards with which the finished product has to comply, but also in the maximum standards that it desires owing to our increasingly more sophisticated way of life. Solutions to building problems must now meet these requirements and are inevitably more complex. A greater amount of scientific and technological knowledge is now available to achieve these complex solutions with the result that an increasing number of specialists are required at various stages of the building process.

This increase in the number of members of the building team has made the co-ordination of their efforts that much more difficult than before. The fact that the majority of these new members are specialists often means that they have had a different training and education from the existing members of the building team. They therefore have difficulty appreciating other areas of the building process and they also have their own specialist language. Communication between individual members of the building team is thus often fraught with misunderstandings; this only serves to exacerbate the problems involved in co-ordinating their efforts.

The above situation is well typified by the emergence of engineering services as a specialism in the building process caused by society's increased demand for the improvement of the internal environment of buildings. The result has been an increased need for a specialist knowledge of services in the design and production of most buildings. This specialism is normally contributed by a consultant at the design stage and a specialist subcontractor during the production stage, although some large organizations do undertake responsibility for both design and production. The very nature of their work requires them to be 'engineer-orientated' and the different languages that result from these different backgrounds can be the cause of many communication problems that arise in the installation of services in the buildings.

Building Services Integration

Attempts to apply traditional management practices and techniques to these problems appear to be becoming less successful as the technical complexity and relative value of services installations increase. Consequently, there is a need to take a fresh look at a problem which is neither wholly technical nor wholly managerial but a combination of both.

This book adopts a systems approach by viewing the building process as a system consisting of technical, organizational and managerial subsystems which themselves are interrelated and subject to contractual constraints.

Chapter 1 provides an overview and defines the problem. Chapter 2 then examines the technical interface between engineering services and the remainder of the building work. The next three chapters continue to investigate this interface in terms of its organizational and managerial characteristics by the application of current thinking in these areas. Chapter 6 discusses the contractual constraints imposed by the standard forms of agreement and contract relevant to engineering services. The final chapter then summarizes issues raised in preceding chapters by setting guidelines for successful integration.

It is not intended to replace or compete with any of the existing textbooks on engineering services, neither should any of the chapters be considered a full treatment of construction technology, management or building contracts. Instead the book should be considered as complementary to existing books in these areas.

Consequently, it should be of assistance to both Main Contractors and Services Subcontractors in performing their roles effectively and also help Architects, Quantity Surveyors and Services Consultants in understanding the problems encountered on building projects and how they can alleviate them. It should also be of value to students of architecture, building, quantity surveying and building services in their study of this important aspect of the design and construction of buildings.

Finally, I would like to express my sincerest thanks to my former colleagues David Highfield who wrote Chapter 2, Barry Fryer who wrote Chapters 3 and 4, and George Fawthrop whose observations were very helpful in writing Chapter 6. I would also like to thank Joanna Barton for her invaluable assistance in typing the original manuscript.

1 · An overview

1.1 Integration or co-ordination?

Integration and co-ordination are terms used in relation to engineering services on building projects, often to mean the same thing. But is this correct? Are the two terms synonymous?

The Oxford English Dictionary defines integration as 'the completion of the whole by the addition of parts' and co-ordination as 'the bringing together of parts into proper relation'. Thus there would seem to be a subtle difference between the two terms. Integration implies a relationship between the parts and the whole, whereas co-ordination implies the interrelationship of the parts themselves.

This is not merely an exercise in semantics but indicates that there is a difference when the terms are applied to engineering services. The integration of engineering services concerns the relationship between engineering services and the remainder of the building project. Conversely, the co-ordination of engineering services concerns the interrelationship of the engineering services themselves. Thus the Architect integrates the work of the Engineering Services Consultant into the design of the project whereas the Engineering Services Consultant co-ordinates the plumbing, heating, electrical and air conditioning services. However this is not to say that the Architect does not co-ordinate. In fact on a larger scale he is responsible for co-ordinating the work of the Engineering Services Consultant, the Structural Engineering Consultant, the Quantity Surveyor and any other specialists necessary to the completion of the design.

The previous discussion serves two purposes. Firstly it defines the terms as they will be used in this book. Secondly, by using the term 'integration' in the title, we have implicitly defined the theme of the book which focuses on the interface between engineering services (i.e. the work carried out by the Nominated Subcontractors) and the processes and procedures normally associated with building work (i.e. work carried out by the Main Contractor or his Domestic Subcontractors during the construction stages of the project).

To summarize, this book is concerned with the relationship between engineering services and the remainder of the building project. Whenever the term 'co-ordination' is used in relation to engineering services it means the interrelationship of plumbing, heating, air conditioning, electrical and any other services on the project. Similarly, when applied to the building project

1

Building Services Integration

itself, co-ordination means the interrelationship of the various specialists involved on the project.

However, before studying the interface between engineering services and the remainder of the building process, let us first look at the building process itself.

1.2 The building process

The building process can be considered as a matrix of conflicting professional and commercial groups combining to contribute their particular specialist skills in order to achieve a desired objective, namely the production of a building. The contributions are often made on a part-time basis and the interests of the various contributors often conflict.

The Tavistock Institute of Human Relations conducted a study of

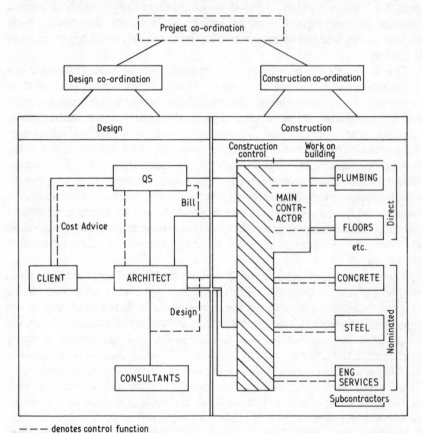

— — — denotes control function

Fig. 1.1 The building process [1]

2

communications in the building industry [1] during the 1960s and as part of that study produced a model of the building process that can provide the basis for the remainder of the discussions in the book.

The model (Fig. 1.1) divided the process into a design function, a construction function and a co-ordinating function. (They defined co-ordination as 'descriptive of the relating together of separate activities and their concerted direction towards a common purpose' – Similar to our definition.)

Within this organization the design function is normally co-ordinated by an Architect. The Architect and all the other members of the design team receive a fee from the Client and are professionally orientated. Furthermore they determine the overall strategy for the project at a relatively small cost. Similarly the construction function is normally co-ordinated by the Main Contractor. Unlike the Architect he is commercially orientated and is only able to make tactical decisions within the strategic constraints set by the design team at a time in the project when the major proportion of the costs are being incurred. The organization, therefore, changes in both structure and orientation during its relatively short life span.

The various members of the organization have allegiances to other building project organizations as well as their own, more stable 'parent' organization. Consequently they are required to resolve conflicts between the short-term objectives of the various building projects to which they may belong and the long-term objectives of their 'parent' organizations. The very nature of their specialist contributions means that the criteria on which they base their decisions differ, e.g. the Architect thinks in terms of shape and form, the Structural Engineer in terms of loads and stresses, the Quantity Surveyor in terms of costs, the Services Engineer in terms of internal environmental considerations and the Main and Subcontractors in terms of production methods. Moreover because the relative importance of the contributions made by these specialists changes as the project progresses, so do the decision-making criteria. Hence, the situation may arise where decisions are being based initially on aesthetic grounds, then in terms of cost and later in terms of production efficiency. This lack of consistency in decision-making criteria can affect the performance of the project organization.

The organization and management of a building project, therefore, requires the co-ordination of a large number of highly differentiated operating units whose roles and interrelationships may change over a relatively short period of time. The fact that these operating units have often had no previous experience of working together merely exacerbates the situation.

1.2.1 Integration during the design stages

A recent study by the Building Research Establishment [2] showed that problems on site caused by the conflicting information on architectural

3

drawings and specialists' drawings are common to most projects and are usually the most disruptive and difficult to deal with. Any improvements in integration during the design stages should, therefore, play a significant part in ensuring effective integration during the entire process. The causes of these problems can be summarized as follows.

(a) Differences in terms of commission

A principal cause of poor integration is the different agreements between the Client and the Architect; and the Client and the Services Consultant. This is discussed in detail in Chapter 6.

(b) The provision of builder's work drawings

The difference in the terms and conditions of agreement mentioned above can also lead to problems involving the provision of builder's work drawings. According to the ACE Conditions of Engagement they are not the responsibility of the Services Consultant since their preparation by him would incur an extra fee. In fact their preparation is normally delegated to the Services Subcontractor who is not always known at the start of a contract. Consequently, the Main Contractor either omits to carry out work necessary for the installation of the services or, in attempting to anticipate the Services Subcontractor's requirements, carries out abortive work. In either case this often results in an increase in project time or cost.

(c) Differences in communication

Another important factor affecting integration during the design stages is the manner in which the information is communicated. The Architect and the Structural Engineer produce pictorial and dimensional drawings in the form of plans, sections and elevations. The Services Consultant, however, communicates by means of diagrammatic presentation since 'working drawings' are not part of his normal service. Consequently, pipelines, ductwork and fittings are not drawn accurately in size or position although such considerations may be of crucial importance to the Structural Engineer, for example, when he is designing a floor slab. This leads to the ever-present problem of holes in slabs being incorrectly located. Similarly the study by the BRE [2], mentioned previously, found that very often, separate drawings are produced for separate services, sometimes to different scales. Obviously this is not conducive to effective integration.

1.2.2 Integration during the construction stages

Recent research carried out at Salford University [3] indicated that one of the major causes of poor integration during construction is the degree of difference between the site personnel of the Main Contractor and the Services

Subcontractors. As mentioned previously, these differences arise because they have allegiances to both the project and to their own 'parent' organizations and can be summarized as follows.

(a) Task

The Main Contractor is concerned with the technical and managerial processes of building and consequently is concerned with terminology, practices and tolerances generally accepted in the building industry. Engineering Services Subcontractors, however, have their roots in the engineering industry and, accordingly, adopt different practices and work to different tolerances. These differences often result in problems involving the location of service fixtures installed by the Services Subcontractor and building elements positioned by the Main Contractor.

(b) Involvement

Services Subcontractors are only involved with projects for relatively short and intermittent periods, whereas the Main Contractor is totally involved from the time he signs the contract until the building is handed over. These differing degrees of involvement affect the criteria upon which they base their decisions. Thus we have the typical situation arising when the Subcontractor's operative is ill and not replaced. This is acceptable to the Subcontractor who will no doubt have the rest of his workforce deployed on other projects. However, as far as the Main Contractor is concerned on this particular project, it could hold up several subsequent operations that would be carried out by his own or other Subcontractor's operatives.

(c) Organization structure

Generally speaking, Main Contractors tend to have a fairly organic structure to cope with the unforeseen problems that may arise on building projects. Engineering Services Subcontractors, however, because of their specialist nature tend to organize themselves in a more rigid way. This results in different levels of responsibility of the respective site personnel, making negotiation difficult.

(d) Social relationships

Engineering Services Subcontractors employ a high proportion of skilled labour on a permanent basis and tend to operate as small organizations. Consequently they normally form very effective social units and, if conditions are unacceptable to them, they may adopt entrenched attitudes based on their prejudices against the Main Contractors. In such situations integration of their work can be difficult. However, if conditions can be made acceptable to them, it will be relatively simple to integrate them into the social system of the site.

Conversely, Main Contractors rely heavily on casual and part-time labour,

5

most of which is semi-skilled. Furthermore, they tend to be larger organizations than the Services Subcontractors. As a result their operatives do not have a similar set of close social interrelationships. Neither do they have as strong a commitment to the goals of either the project or the parent organization. This lack of social cohesion between the two groups of operatives in turn affects any technical interdependence of their site operations.

1.2.3 The design/construction interface

Apart from the differences between the design team and the construction team mentioned previously, a major problem associated with the design/ construction interface is the accepted practice of nomination of the Services Subcontractor by the Architect.

Nominated Subcontractors are seldom appointed at the same time as the Main Contractor. They may be appointed before the Main Contractor, in which case any planning of their work, upon which they may have based their estimate, cannot have taken into consideration the Main Contractor's overall planning policy for the project. Any discrepancies between the Nominated Subcontractor's plan and the Main Contractor's plan can, therefore, be a source of integration problems throughout the project.

Alternatively, the Nominated Subcontractor may not be appointed until work has started on site with the result that errors or omissions in the work may arise because the Main Contractor is not fully aware of the Nominated Subcontractor's requirements.

In either of the above situations the problems are exacerbated by the special relationship that exists between the Nominated Subcontractor and the Architect; although the Nominated Subcontractor is less subject to the Main Contractor's authority than the direct Subcontractor, his attitude is often modified by the need for any future work that the Architect may provide.

1.2.4 Alternative contractual relationships

More recently, alternative forms of contractual relationships, e.g. negotiated contracts, package deals and project management, have been devised to alleviate some of the problems outlined above. In principle they all attempt to break down the barrier between the design function and the production function that is present with the traditional practices of open- and selective-tendering. As such they do not necessarily have a direct effect on services integration, although there could be an indirect effect in view of the fact that project communications tend to be improved.

1.3 A framework for integration

From the foregoing discussions, it can be seen that the integration of engineering services on building projects is affected by technical, organizational and managerial factors, and operates within contractual constraints. These factors are themselves interrelated and therefore affect the building project in a complex manner.

Consequently, if engineering services are to be successfully integrated on building projects, then their relationship with the remainder of the building project must be considered in terms of technical, organizational, managerial and contractual factors.

The remaining chapters of this book will cover these factors in more detail and finally provide guidelines for successful integration.

References

(1) Higgin, G. and Jessop N. (1965) *Communications in the Building Industry*, Tavistock Publications, London.
(2) Crawshaw, D. (1977) Co-ordinating working drawings – the role of site management. *Building Technology and Management*, **15th February**, pp. 13–15 and 25.
(3) Barton, P.K. (1976) *The co-ordination of mechanical and electrical services subcontractors within the building process*, MSc thesis, Salford University.

2 · *Technical aspects*

2.1 Factors affecting design

The techniques used to incorporate engineering services within the structure and fabric of a building depend upon a number of variable factors; some of the more important considerations affecting services integration are discussed below.

2.1.1 Building type

The services requirements of different buildings, and therefore their incorporation, may vary significantly. For example, a hospital, with its operating theatres and treatment rooms needing precisely controlled environmental conditions, will present a far more complex problem with regard to services integration than an office building or a warehouse.

2.1.2 Size and shape of building

The size and shape of a building can significantly affect the way in which services are integrated and distributed. A multi-storey office building, where all of the activities requiring servicing are concentrated in a relatively small plan area, will require a different approach to the incorporation of its services from a large school comprising several separated low-rise blocks over a wide area. In the case of the multi-storey office building, there will be a large number of vertical service runs and horizontal service runs, the latter being relatively short in length. In the case of the school, there will be very few vertical service runs and many long horizontal runs between and within different buildings, particularly if appliances in those buildings are all served by centralized plant.

2.1.3 Type of construction

Certain types of building construction lend themselves more easily to the incorporation of engineering services. One such example is the fairly common form of construction based upon a service core. The service core can be designed as a major vertical structural element, and constructed first; the remainder of the building's structural framework would be subsequently

8

erected around it. Alternatively, the service core may be a non-structural element constructed with or after the main structural framework. In either case, the service core provides a suitable, spacious vertical zone within the building envelope for accommodation of most of the vertical service runs and much of the services plant required in the building.

2.1.4   Other design features of the building

The use of certain features within the building can help solve many of the problems relating to services location, distribution and concealment. Suspended-ceilings, raised-floors and hollow-partitioning systems are some examples of design features which can provide a ready solution to incorporation of engineering services.

2.1.5   The number of different services

The number of different services needing to be incorporated within the building envelope will depend to a large extent upon the building type. Where a large number of services are required, the problems relating to their integration will be more complex, and more thought will have to be given to their location, distribution and concealment at the design stage. A greater number of suitable locations will have to be considered and incorporated into the design, and the problems of numerous service runs competing for limited zones of space must be given careful consideration.

It should also be appreciated that the number and nature of services within a particular building can be varied, therefore reducing, or adding to, the problems of their incorporation. For example, the designer of a multi-storey office building may elect to use a simple hot-water radiator heating system in conjunction with openable windows as a means of controlling the internal environment, in preference to a sophisticated mechanical air-conditioning system involving the use of complex plant and bulky ductwork. It is clear that the former system, with its small-diameter pipework and simpler plant and appliances, will be much simpler to incorporate and conceal than the latter system.

In general, the more complicated the function of a building and the activities within it, the more extensive and varied will be its services, and before their actual incorporation within the building is described, it is essential to consider the categories and nature of services likely to be met in most buildings.

2.2   Categories of engineering services

Engineering services and the items they serve can be conveniently subdivided into three elements:

Building Services Integration

Plant and equipment
Service runs
Appliances

and many comprise all three elements. For example, an electric typewriter (appliance) in a large office building relies for its power and operation upon a system of electrical sub-circuits and large-capacity distribution cables (service runs) and, in turn, a local- and a main-distribution board (plant and equipment). Some categories of engineering services, however, may only have two elements. For example, if an appliance is immediately adjacent to its plant room, a service run will not be necessary.

The following lists include most of the engineering services elements likely to be found in a wide range of buildings.

2.2.1 Plant and equipment

(a) Electrical distribution boards
(b) Telephone switchboards
(c) Electricity generating plant
(d) Air-conditioning plant
(e) Lift motor rooms
(f) Escalator motors
(g) Water-heating plant (boilers)
(h) Water-pumping equipment (for high-rise buildings)
(i) Water-storage cisterns

2.2.2 Service runs

(a) Electrical distribution cables and wiring systems to plant and to appliances
(b) Telephone cables and wiring systems
(c) Air-conditioning ductwork
(d) Cold-water supply pipework to:
    cisterns
    appliances
    boiler plant
    air-conditioning plant
    other plant and machinery
(e) Cold-water supply pipework for firefighting services including:
    wet risers
    dry risers
    sprinkler systems
    hose reels
(f) Hot-water supply pipework to plant and equipment, machinery and appliances

10

(g) Waste pipework from sanitary appliances, and plant and machinery
(h) Gas supply pipework to gas-fired plant and machinery, boilers and appliances
(i) Specialist gas supplies (in hospitals)
(j) Fuel supply pipework to plant and machinery, boilers and appliances
(k) Refuse chutes (for high-rise buildings)

2.2.3   Appliances

(a) Light fittings
(b) Electrical office equipment, including:
   typewriters
   calculators
   minicomputers
   video display units
(c) Heating appliances including:
   radiators
   convectors
   storage heaters, etc.
(d) Telephones
(e) Closed-circuit television equipment
(f) Other telecommunications equipment including:
   loudspeakers
   teleprinters
   staff location systems
   bell equipment, etc.
(g) Sanitary appliances including:
   baths
   showers
   sinks and washbasins
   WCs, etc.
(h) Instantaneous localized water-heaters
(i) Industrial machinery
(j) Lifts
(k) Escalators
(l) Air-conditioning terminals

2.3 The nature of engineering services

In addition to the more general factors affecting the incorporation of engineering services discussed in Section 2.1, the specific nature of the various services will be of vital importance in determining how they are integrated, distributed and concealed. Defining the nature of engineering services is not a

11

simple matter, since it depends upon a number of aspects which are discussed below.

2.3.1 Size

The sizes of plant, service runs and appliances will significantly affect the choice of suitable locations and methods of distribution within the building. The number of suitable locations for electrical wiring circuits will, for example, far exceed the number of suitable locations for air-conditioning ductwork.

2.3.2 Shape

The shape of the services element being considered may affect its positioning and relationship with the structure, finishes and other services.

2.3.3 Weight

The weight of services elements can dictate the means used to incorporate them into the building. This is particularly true for heavy services plant and equipment which will impose high loading on the building's structure, requiring localized strengthening of the structure in areas where plant rooms are to be located. Certain types of ductwork and pipework are fairly heavy and due consideration should be given to the design of structural floors where a large amount of ductwork and pipework, etc, is to be suspended from them.

2.3.4 Compatibility of services

In certain cases, it may not be desirable to locate incompatible service runs adjacent to each other. The positioning of electrical wiring runs close to pipework carrying liquids and should be avoided if possible. If this is unavoidable, the electrical service should be vertically above any liquid-carrying pipework. Pipelines containing inflammable gases or fuels should be located in the least vulnerable positions with regard to explosion risks. 'Hot' service runs should not be located immediately adjacent to service runs containing fluids which must remain cold, unless proper insulation is provided.

2.3.5 Insulation and additional fittings

Certain service runs may have to be provided with thermal insulation or have additional fittings incorporated such as valves, joint flanges, access points, etc. In such cases, the overall size and shape of the service run may be very different from the basic pipe or duct, and it is essential that, if this is likely to occur, it is considered at as early a stage as possible in the design process.

2.3.6 Noise and vibration

The problems of noise and vibration often affect services incorporation where plant and equipment are concerned. Lift motors, air-conditioning plant, pumping equipment and boilers may be very noisy during operation, and it is essential that they are located away from rooms where relative quietness is important. The provision of adequate sound insulation to plant rooms must also be given careful consideration at design stage. In addition to noise, certain plant may produce vibrations which can be transmitted throughout the building and which may inflict structural damage, unless attention is paid to the provision of adequate mountings designed to suppress vibrations, and suitable breaks in the structure to prevent vibration transmission.

Some of the general and specific factors affecting the incorporation of service within the building envelope have now been considered. Another important constraint, which is dealt with in detail later in this chapter, should be mentioned at this point; this concerns the effect of the Building Regulations upon services incorporation.

Several parts of the Building Regulations have an important effect upon the integration, distribution and concealment of engineering services and, because they are in the form of statutory requirements, they are better described as design constraints. The effects upon the incorporation of services by the Buildings Regulations (1976) will be considered in Section 2.6.

2.4 Location of engineering services within the building

During the design of a building, the Architect, in consultation with a specialist Services Engineer, must decide on the categories and nature of the engineering services required. This will include most or some of the services categories listed in Section 2.2, depending upon the complexity of the building. Having reached this stage, and having considered the more specific nature of the various services, it must then be decided how these services are to be integrated with the building structure and finishes and how they are to be concealed.

When deciding upon how to incorporate services, the designer will be aware of the fact that some have a greater flexibility of location than others. This is particularly true of service runs; in general, the smaller the size of the service run, the greater will be the number of possible locations. For example, electrical wiring to desktop machinery can be located in trunking within the floor structure or screed, within hollow partitions, in hollow skirting trunking, or in the suspended ceiling. On the other hand, runs of bulky air-conditioning ducting can usually only be located within deep suspended-ceiling voids and special service ducts.

Building Services Integration

2.4.1 Location of plant, equipment and appliances

With regard to the service elements at each end of the service runs (i.e. plant and equipment, and appliances) their locations tend to be less flexible. For example, the location of lifts and sanitary appliances will be dictated by the building's circulation arrangements and where the building users are located during working hours. Lift motor rooms and water-storage cisterns will normally be located at the bottom or the top of the building and, if necessary, water-pumping plant will be located in the basement or at ground level. As well as being less positionally flexible, major items of services plant and equipment will have large portions of the building left free specifically for their location, usually in the form of specially constructed plant rooms.

It is clear, therefore, that the location of plant and equipment, and, in most cases, the appliances served, is a more clear-cut decision than that for service runs; it is the incorporation of service runs which is considered in the next section. Since it is intended that a wide range of building types should be covered, the methods described have been selected as being generally applicable to a number of different building types rather than concentrating upon one particular category of building. The suitability of various methods to particular categories of building will, however, be included where applicable.

2.4.2 Locations for service runs

The following list gives the possible locations for service runs within a building. (It should be borne in mind, however, that the suitability of a particular location for a particular service run will depend upon a number of factors, particularly those discussed in Section 2.3.)

(a) Suspended ceilings:
     void above (suspended from structure)
     within ceiling
     suspended from ceiling
(b) Within roof void:
     between roof structure and ceiling, or
     with portal frames and triangulated trusses, a large triangular void may be available
(c) On top of roof
(d) Within floor structure:
     hollow floor units
     cast-in ducts
     floor-trunking
(e) Within floor screed (floor-trunking embedded into the screed)
(f) Raised floors (provide a void under whole area similar to a suspended-ceiling void)

14

(g) Skirtings (pre-formed metal or plastic skirting sections)
(h) Within wall structure (cast-in ducts, conduit)
(i) Hollow partitions
(j) Fixed to face of internal and external walls (may be on outside of building)
(k) Vertical service core
    structural or non-structural
    may be designed to contain all or most of the building's vertical service runs
(l) Service ducts
    specially-designed vertical or horizontal ducts to take a number of service runs
    'walk-in' ducts
    subdivisions of service core
    underground service ducts
(m) Service floors (structural service floors may be a full-storey height between each floor where services are numerous, complex and bulky).

(a) Suspended ceilings

The suspended ceiling, more than any other interior design feature, has been the panacea for many problems concerning services integration in recent years. The suspension of an artificial ceiling from the main floor or roof structure provides an attractive finish and, more importantly, a useful spacious void over the whole building area for the location of a large number of different service runs. The depth of a suspended ceiling void can be varied within a wide range of limits, the controlling factors being the maximum size of any services to be concealed and the maximum overall storey height required. A typical solution for an office building would be as follows:

Overall storey height	3.100 m
comprising:	
room height	2.450 m
suspended ceiling void	0.500 m
floor slab and finish	0.150 m

A suspended ceiling void, 0.5 m in depth, would cater for the incorporation of several different services. Greater void depths are possible if the architect reduces the room height to the minimum permitted by the Building Regulations Part K.8 (i.e. 2.3 m), or if the storey height is increased.

The principal advantage of the suspended ceiling is that all of the horizontal service runs listed in Section 2.2.2 can be incorporated within it. If this is the case, however, it is essential that careful thought be given to co-ordination of the services design and installation in order to avoid problems arising from 'overcrowding' and the probability of a large number of service runs competing for the limited space available.

Building Services Integration

An important consideration in the design of suspended-ceiling systems is the use of adequate fire-stopping at strategic intervals within the void. There have been many cases recently where buildings have been gutted by fire due to the 'short-circuiting' of compartment walls by suspended ceilings. Once a fire reaches the ceiling void, it can spread rapidly through the whole building if suitable fire-stops are not available. A further consideration where fire-stops are necessary is that the various service runs will have to pass through them without reducing their prime function of preventing the passage of fire. The use of fire-stops is considered in detail later in this chapter.

A very wide range of proprietary suspended-ceiling systems are available today, ranging from relatively simple grid systems to complex integrated ceilings which are specifically designed to incorporate various services and appliances in their range of components.

The simplest suspended-ceiling systems comprise a main and secondary grid suspended from the soffit of the floor above by metal wires or hangers. The ceiling tiles are supported by this horizontal grid, which may be concealed or exposed according to the system used. Provision is made for the incorporation of light fittings, air-conditioning grilles, etc.

The more complex integrated ceilings, which have been introduced more recently, comprise a fully integrated, dimensionally co-ordinated range of fittings and appliances for lighting, air conditioning, etc., in addition to the basic grid suspension system. A typical proprietary integrated suspended-ceiling system would include the following components:

- (i) Metal hangers
- (ii) Main and secondary suspension grids
- (iii) Ceiling boxes for fixing or connection of lighting fittings and diffusers
- (iv) Supply air terminals
- (v) Air exhaust boxes
- (vi) Air supply and exhaust grilles
- (vii) Linear air-diffusers
- (viii) Ducting adaptor boxes for linking supply and exhaust terminals to main air-conditioning ductwork
- (ix) Lightweight trunking and accessories
- (x) A range of ceiling tiles to suit the interior-design requirements

Sequence of operations
In order to co-ordinate the services installation within the building programme, the three contractors involved – mechanical (M), electrical (E) and ceiling (C) – must maintain good communications and co-operate closely with each other; the sequence of operations should normally be as shown in Fig. 2.1 and listed below. (The numbers on Fig. 2.1 correspond to the order of operations.)

16

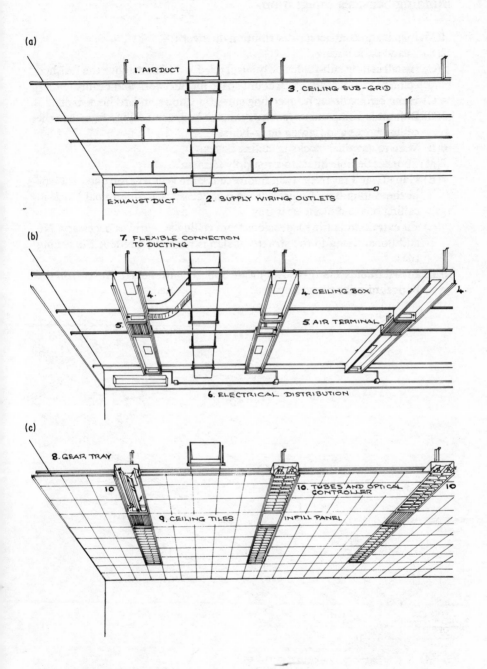

(a)

1. AIR DUCT
3. CEILING SUB-GRID
EXHAUST DUCT
2. SUPPLY WIRING OUTLETS

(b)

7. FLEXIBLE CONNECTION TO DUCTING
4. CEILING BOX
4.
5. AIR TERMINAL
5.
6. ELECTRICAL DISTRIBUTION

(c)

8. GEAR TRAY
10
10. TUBES AND OPTICAL CONTROLLER
10
9. CEILING TILES
INFILL PANEL

Fig. 2.1 Integrated suspended ceiling installation sequence (by courtesy of Thorn Lighting Ltd)

Building Services Integration

1(M) Install and connect air-distribution ductwork.

2(E) Install basic wiring.

3(C) Install ceiling sub-grid rigidly suspended at 145 mm above the finished ceiling level, taking into account space for ductwork and beams.

4(C) Hang ceiling boxes from ceiling sub-grid using standard hook-bolts.

5(C) Bolt other components, such as exhaust boxes and ceiling frames to the ceiling boxes and tighten hook-bolts.

6(E) Wire to terminal blocks in ceiling boxes.

7(M) Connect flexible ducts to air-supply terminals.

8(E) Hang Gear Trays (e.g. twin fluorescent lamp gear tray) on one wire-way in the ceiling box. Connect leads from gear trays to terminal block in ceiling box and locate gear tray.

9(C) Fit extra ceiling tile suspensions from ceiling sub-grid as necessary. No additional fixing to the structural slab is normally needed. Fix ceiling tiles.

10(E) Install fluorescent tubes and locate optical controllers (diffusers) on the flanges of ceiling boxes.

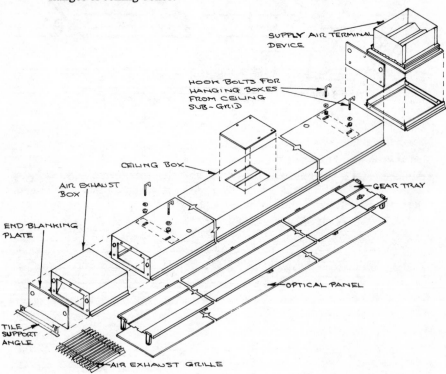

Fig. 2.2 Integrated suspended ceiling – exploded diagram of ceiling box components (by courtesy of Thorn Lighting Ltd)

18

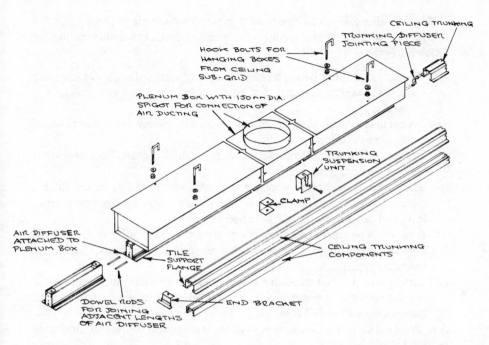

Fig. 2.3 Integrated suspended ceiling – exploded diagram of linear air-diffuser and lightweight trunking components (by courtesy of Thorn Lighting Ltd)

(b) Raised floors

Raised floors provide a space suitable for housing service runs similar in nature to that provided by suspended ceilings. A number of proprietary systems are available, providing a 'false' floor some distance above the structural floor with a useful void beneath suitable for housing a wide range of services. Raised floor voids, like suspended ceiling voids, can also be used as plenum chambers for air distribution. Proprietary raised floor systems are suitable for computer rooms, control rooms, automatic telephone exchanges, offices and a wide range of other applications. Floor panels are usually timber or steel supported by adjustable steel props. Access to the void beneath may be over the whole area of the floor, with all panels being removable, or restricted access via strategically located removable panels. Panel sizes are modular, 600×600 mm, 1200×600 mm and 2400×600 mm being the most popular. The structural floor supporting a raised floor does not have to be perfectly level or smooth, since support props are adjustable to cater for discrepancies. Thus, finishing operations such as power floating or screeding can be omitted, resulting in cost savings in the structural floor construction. Most proprietary systems produce a void depth up to 1 m which allows for incorporation of the bulkiest service runs.

19

Building Services Integration

When evaluating raised floors as a means of concealing service runs in comparison with suspended ceilings, the building designer should consider the following points:

(i) The structural floor beneath provides a ready means of support for service runs, whereas with suspended ceilings, some form of suspension system is necessary.

(ii) Access to the void is simpler and safer than with suspended ceilings, where ladders are necessary.

(iii) Support of the raised floor itself directly off the structural floor beneath is simpler and quicker.

(iv) The cost of providing an accurate, smooth finish to the structural floor is eliminated since support props are designed to cater for discrepancies in level and can also be tilted where necessary.

(v) A raised floor must possess sufficient strength and rigidity to support the normal superimposed floor loads, including occupants, furniture, machinery, etc.

(vi) Service runs located beneath a raised floor must be co-ordinated to avoid the support props which are larger and often more closely spaced than hangers for suspended ceilings.

A typical proprietary raised flooring system is described below and illustrated in Figs 2.4 and 2.5.

(i) Floor panels
- $600 \times 600 \times 54.5$ mm deep, heavy-gauge galvanized pressed steel with 30 mm thick high-density processed timber insulating core;
- Supported at each corner by adjustable props and lock in position without screwing or bolting;
- Full access possible by raising panels with special lifting devices;
- Panel surface may be finished with PVC, linoleum, carpet, plastic laminate or other suitable finish to the client's requirements.

(ii) Support props
- Support capabilities range from general office loads to heavy plant loads such as computers. Maximum uniformly distributed load: 24 kN m^{-2}. Maximum point load: 4.4 kN (over a 25 mm square);
- Props comprise 27 mm diameter galvanized steel tube with die-cast aluminium castellated head and 114 mm diameter base plate for adhesive- or screw-fixing to sub-floor;
- Capable of adjustment to $\pm$ 19 mm to cater for variation in sub-floor levels;
- Special tilting base plates available to ensure fullest contact with uneven sub-floor surfaces whilst maintaining props truly vertical.

20

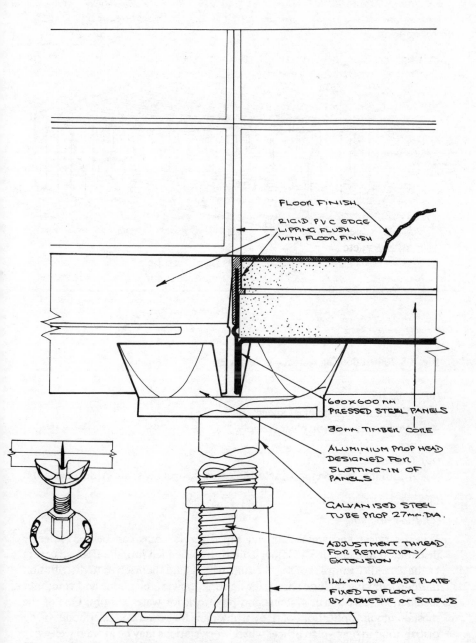

FLOOR FINISH.

RIGID PVC EDGE
LIPPING FLUSH
WITH FLOOR FINISH

600×600 mm
PRESSED STEEL PANELS

30mm TIMBER CORE

ALUMINIUM PROP HEAD
DESIGNED FOR
SLOTTING-IN OF
PANELS

GALVANISED STEEL
TUBE PROP 27mm DIA.

ADJUSTMENT THREAD
FOR RETRACTION/
EXTENSION

144mm DIA BASE PLATE
FIXED TO FLOOR
BY ADHESIVE or SCREWS

Fig. 2.4 Details of raised flooring system (by courtesy of Propaflor Ltd)

Building Services Integration

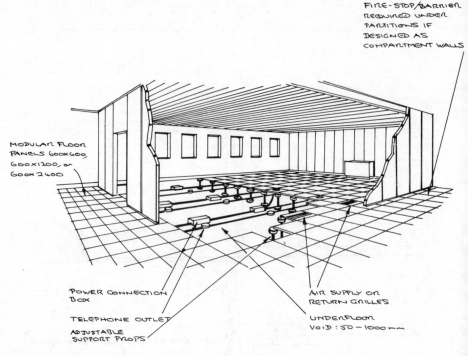

FIRE-STOP/BARRIER
REQUIRED UNDER
PARTITIONS IF
DESIGNED AS
COMPARTMENT WALLS

MODULAR FLOOR
PANELS 600x600,
600x1200, or
600x2400

POWER CONNECTION
BOX

TELEPHONE OUTLET

ADJUSTABLE
SUPPORT PROPS

AIR SUPPLY OR
RETURN GRILLES

UNDERFLOOR
VOID : 50 – 1000 mm

Fig. 2.5 Raised flooring system – general view

(iii) Void size
–   Minimum: 75 mm clear space
–   Maximum: 914 mm clear space

(iv) General
–   Additional components include skirtings, upstands, air grilles, cut-outs, etc.

(c) Floor-trunking

Wired services and small-diameter piped service runs can be conveniently distributed in metal or PVC floor-trunking embedded into the floor structure or the screed. Examples of service runs which lend themselves to distribution in floor-trunking include wiring for lighting, power, telephone and computer installations, fire alarm systems and pipework for water supply. One of the most common applications of floor-trunking is for power and telephone wiring distribution in open-plan offices where work stations may be located well away from perimeter and partition walls. In this case, floor-trunking avoids the necessity of having to trail loose cables from perimeter socket outlets to isolated

22

office machinery and telephones, with the associated risks to personnel that this would involve.

Floor-trunking is generally available with single, double or triple compartments, typical sizes being:

Single compartment: 75 mm wide ×25, 38 or 50 mm deep
Double compartment: 150 mm wide ×25, 38 or 50 mm deep
Triple compartment: 225 mm wide ×25, 38 or 50 mm deep

Where bulkier service runs, such as insulated pipework, need to be concealed, trunking up to 150 mm deep is available. Clearly, trunking of this depth cannot be accommodated within the screed and at least part of the depth must be set into the floor structure itself.

Generally, floor-trunking and its accessories are manufactured from zinc-coated mild steel 1–2 mm thick. Other suitable materials include extruded unplasticized PVC.

It is essential to integrate the planning of the floor-trunking and the positions of associated services outlets to suit the proposed layout of the spaces being serviced. This is necessary to avoid the trunking runs and outlets conflicting with partitions, door openings, corridors, other services and the like. In certain building types, this may, however, be difficult, for example in open plan offices for speculative rental. In such cases, the internal layout will not be known when the services are installed and thus the planning of trunking runs and outlets should allow as much flexibility as possible in the location of work-stations, fixtures, fittings, partitions, etc.

Floor-trunking systems of the types described in this section are generally limited to use in conjunction with in-situ concrete floor construction, or precast concrete flooring where a topping screed of sufficient thickness is applied.

Three basic forms of floor-trunking are generally available and they differ mainly in terms of the degree of accessibility to the service runs they conceal.

The first form of floor-trunking is laid on the structural floor slab and surrounded and covered over by the screed. Access is restricted to strategically placed inspection boxes and service outlet boxes.

A typical example of this form of floor-trunking is illustrated in Fig. 2.6 and described below:

(i) Trunking
Manufactured from 1.6 mm zinc-coated mild steel. Base plate and body welded together to form a single unit with central divider producing two compartments.

(ii) Sizes
Available in two sizes:

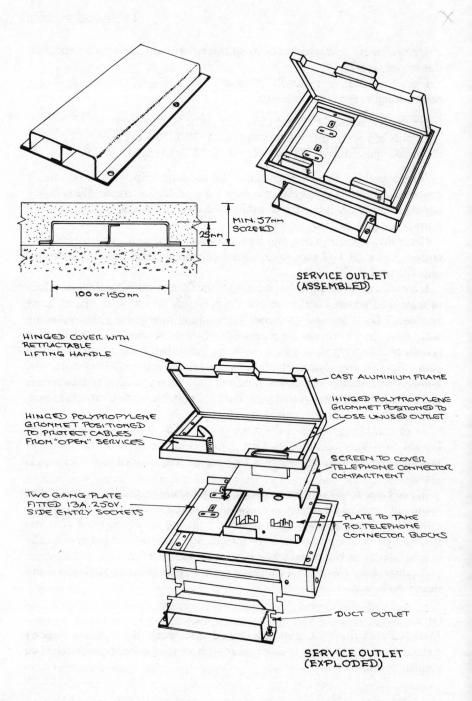

MIN. 57mm
SCREED

25mm

100 or 150mm

SERVICE OUTLET
(ASSEMBLED)

HINGED COVER WITH
RETRACTABLE
LIFTING HANDLE

CAST ALUMINIUM FRAME

HINGED POLYPROPYLENE
GROMMET POSITIONED TO
CLOSE UNUSED OUTLET

HINGED POLYPROPYLENE
GROMMET POSITIONED
TO PROTECT CABLES
FROM "OPEN" SERVICES

SCREEN TO COVER
TELEPHONE CONNECTOR
COMPARTMENT

TWO GANG PLATE
FITTED 13A. 250V.
SIDE ENTRY SOCKETS

PLATE TO TAKE
P.O. TELEPHONE
CONNECTOR BLOCKS

DUCT OUTLET

SERVICE OUTLET
(EXPLODED)

Fig. 2.6 Floor-trunking system (by courtesy of Walsall Conduits Ltd)

100 mm wide (2×50 mm compartments) × 25 mm deep

150 mm wide (2×75 mm compartments) × 25 deep.

(iii) Fittings

Fittings available include vertical bends, for connecting horizontal runs to vertical runs, expansion joints, stop-ends, straight connectors, inspection boxes and service outlet boxes.

(iv) Installation

Lengths of trunking are positioned on the structural floor slab and the screed, minimum thickness 57 mm (giving a 32 mm cover over the trunking), is laid around and over it. Lateral movement of the trunking whilst screeding must be avoided. This can be done by bedding it on a layer of sand and cement which will also facilitate levelling. Alternatively, the trunking may be screwed or shot-fired to the structural floor.

(v) Inspection Boxes

Inspection boxes are supplied with a cast aluminium frame and a reversible recessed tray cover designed to cater for two thicknesses of floor covering – 3 mm or 6 mm. These boxes can be positioned at any location in a trunking run using special connectors. The frame projects above the trunking so that the recessed tray cover is at floor finish level. The cover is secured by four corner screws which facilitate its easy removal for access to the trunking compartments.

(vi) Service outlet boxes

Supplies with a cast aluminium frame and a recessed hinged tray with retractable lifting handle. As with the inspection box, the tray can take either a 3 mm or 6 mm thickness of floor covering. The box contains two service plates, one fitted with two 13 A socket outlets; the other designed to receive Post Office telephone connector blocks.

A variation of this system provides greater flexibility of installation by offering a wider range of sizes and number of compartments as illustrated in Fig. 2.7 and described below.

It is available in single, double or triple compartment format, 75, 150 and 225 mm wide respectively. Each is manufactured in three standard depths – 25, 38 or 50 mm. Fittings and installation are similar to the above, with the exception that a greater screed-thickness, or partial letting-into the floor structure, will be necessary with the deeper sections. Inspection boxes are available for installation at any position and are provided with recessed trays to suit any depth of floor finish. Service outlets comprise metal floor pedestals fixed to the trunking by means of internally threaded duct outlets.

Building Services Integration

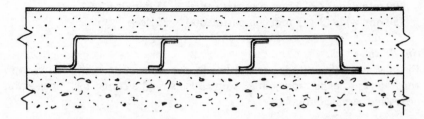

Fig. 2.7 Alternative floor-trunking system (by courtesy of Walsall Conduits Ltd)

The second form of floor-trunking is laid on the structural floor slab and surrounded, but not covered, by the screed. Access is possible along the full length of the trunking via continuous removable flat covers flush with the top of the screed. Floor coverings are laid directly over the top of the trunking covers and have to be lifted if access to the trunking is required.

A typical example of this form of trunking is illustrated in Fig. 2.8 and described below.

(i) Trunking

Body manufactured from 1.6 mm zinc coated mild steel with central divider to form twin compartments. Cover manufactured from 3 mm zinc-coated mild steel and secured to body with countersunk screws. Bonded neoprene cork strip fitted on trunking flange to cushion the cover and provide a dust seal. Standard length: 2 m, with one connector per length plus a pair of fixing feet incorporating levelling screws.

(ii) Sizes

Standard size: 258 mm wide × 57 mm deep. Other depths can be manufactured as required.

(iii) Fittings

Fittings available include connectors for joining horizontal runs to vertical runs, stop-ends, straight connectors, fixing feet with levelling screws, inspection boxes and service outlets.

(iv) Installation

Lengths of trunking are positioned on the structural slab and the 57 mm screed laid around them to level flush with the cover plate. It is essential that the cover plate is screwed down and the screw holes greased before screeding. This enables the screed to be finished flush with the cover plate more easily and prevents flow of screed into the trunking and screw holes. The screws should not be withdrawn until the screed has hardened. A pair of steel angle fixing feet with adjustable levelling screws per 2 m length of trunking facilitates accurate

26

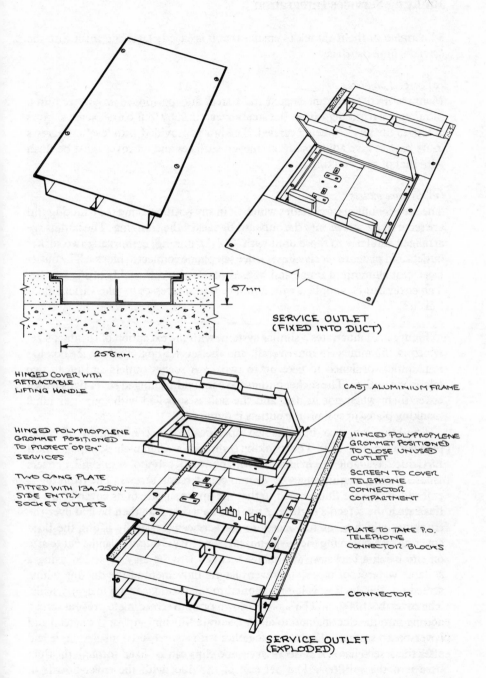

57mm

258mm

SERVICE OUTLET
(FIXED INTO DUCT)

HINGED COVER WITH
RETRACTABLE
LIFTING HANDLE

CAST ALUMINIUM FRAME

HINGED POLYPROPYLENE
GROMMET POSITIONED
TO PROTECT "OPEN"
SERVICES

HINGED POLYPROPYLENE
GROMMET POSITIONED
TO CLOSE UNUSED
OUTLET

TWO GANG PLATE
FITTED WITH 13A. 250V.
SIDE ENTRY
SOCKET OUTLETS

SCREEN TO COVER
TELEPHONE
CONNECTOR
COMPARTMENT

PLATE TO TAKE P.O.
TELEPHONE
CONNECTOR BLOCKS

CONNECTOR

SERVICE OUTLET
(EXPLODED)

Fig. 2.8 Alternative floor-trunking system (by courtesy of Walsall Conduits Ltd)

Building Services Integration

adjustment of the trunking to ensure that it is exactly level and flush with the
screed's upper surface.

(v) Inspection boxes
Manufactured from zinc-coated mild steel and positioned in any required
location in a trunking run. A flat steel cover, fixed by four corner screws, gives
access to the services being carried. The box is provided with levelling screws
in its base to give adjustment on uneven surfaces and its cover must be flush
with that of the trunking.

(vi) Service outlets
The services outlets are cradles which fit in any position along the trunking and
are secured by screws into the outward flanges of the trunking. The outlets are
arranged similarly to those used with 'C.81' trunking, comprising two socket
outlets and plates to receive Post Office telephone connector blocks. The outlet
has a cast aluminium frame and hinged cover with retractable lifting handle.
The cover can be supplied with 3 mm or 6 mm recesses to take various floor
finishes.

Figure 2.10 illustrates a similar system, with the exception of the duct size,
which is 162 mm × 38 mm overall, and the service box. The service box has
four outlets designed to take up to two 13 A socket outlets and up to two
telephone outlets. The socket outlets have individual hinged cover flaps which
cover them when not in use, and the unit is supplied with four individual
blanking plates to seal off the outlets if required.

Trunking can also be obtained specifically for concealment of water
pipework (see Fig. 2.9). The trunking comprises a 1.5 mm-thick unplasticized
PVC duct, available in 3 m lengths, with plywood, asbestolux or similar covers
secured to the duct's flanges by 25 mm countersunk screws. The trunking is
embedded into the floor screed so that the upper surface of its cover-boards is
flush with the screed's surface. Any floor covering may then be laid over the
trunking, which gives full access to the services carried by lifting the floor
covering and removing the cover-boards. The uPVC ducting can be cut to size
on site using a hacksaw, and joints between lengths may be sealed using a
suitable waterproof tape. To prevent lateral movement of the ducting whilst
screeding, the ducting is lightly pinned to the subfloor using masonry nails.
The cover-boards should be screwed down prior to screeding to prevent screed
getting into the ducting and to allow accurate 'flushing-up' of the screed and
cover-board surfaces. Pipework, together with any required insulation, is laid
after the screed has set. If necessary, pipe clips can be fixed through the duct
base into the subfloor. The net size of the duct with the cover-boards in
position is 100 mm wide × 36.5 mm deep.

The third form of floor trunking also gives continuous access via covers

28

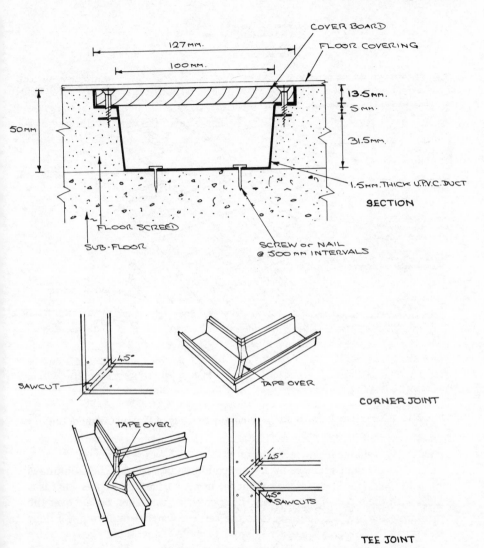

Fig. 2.9 Floor-ducting system (by courtesy of Westbrick Plastics Ltd)

which are flush with the top of the screed. It differs from the types previously described in that the covers comprise shallow trays which are 'filled' with the floor finish. The metal edging to the cover trays is always visible, but it has the advantage that access is quicker and simpler since there is no need to lift large areas of floor covering to gain access to the duct. A system of this type is described below and illustrated in Fig. 2.11.

29

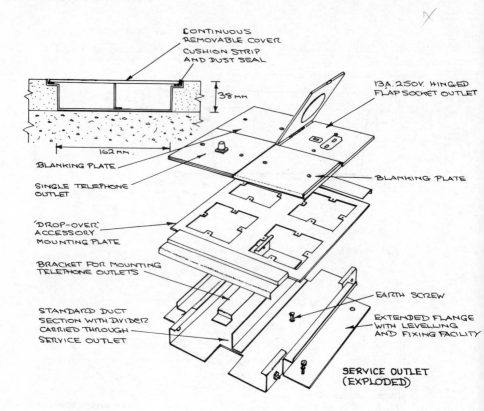

CONTINUOUS
REMOVABLE COVER
CUSHION STRIP
AND DUST SEAL

13A. 250V. HINGED
FLAP SOCKET OUTLET

38mm

162mm.

BLANKING PLATE

SINGLE TELEPHONE
OUTLET

BLANKING PLATE

'DROP-OVER'
ACCESSORY
MOUNTING PLATE

BRACKET FOR MOUNTING
TELEPHONE OUTLETS

EARTH SCREW

STANDARD DUCT
SECTION WITH DIVIDER
CARRIED THROUGH
SERVICE OUTLET

EXTENDED FLANGE
WITH LEVELLING
AND FIXING FACILITY

SERVICE OUTLET
(EXPLODED)

Fig. 2.10 Alternative floor-trunking system (by courtesy of Walsall Conduits Ltd)

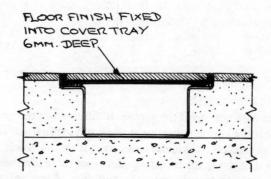

FLOOR FINISH FIXED
INTO COVER TRAY
6mm. DEEP.

Fig. 2.11 Alternative floor-trunking system (by courtesy of Walsall Conduits Ltd)

(i) Trunking
Manufactured from 1.6 mm zinc-coated mild steel and supplied in 2 m lengths. Dividers can be fitted if required. The cover trays have a standard 6 mm recess and alternative depths are available to order. The covers are cushioned by a bonded neoprene cork strip on the trunking flange, which also acts as a dust seal.

(ii) Sizes
The trunking is available in a wide range of sizes, 50–150 mm wide and 50–150 mm deep.

(iii) Fittings
The fittings available include angles, tees, crosses, side and end outlets, stop-ends and connectors.

Floor-trunking layouts
Floor-trunking offers a great deal of flexibility in the planning and installation of wired and piped services, with a wide range of proprietary systems available to cater for most requirements. Varying degrees of access to the service runs carried are also possible, from the very limited access at strategic points via inspection boxes and outlet boxes, to the 100% access over the trunking's full length via 'lift-out' floor trays. Wired and piped services can be taken to any number of points in any position throughout the entire area of the building in an efficient, convenient and invisible distribution system. Figure 2.13 shows a typical floor-trunking distribution system for electrical and telephone wiring in a part open-plan, part partitioned office building. The electrical supply enters each floor level from a vertical services duct at one end of the building and wiring is run from the distribution board into the underfloor trunking network. The telephone riser enters at the opposite end of the building, also in a vertical services duct. Telephone wiring is then run into the same multi-compartmented floor trunking network as the electrical wiring and conveyed, with the electrical wiring, throughout the building.

(d) Skirting trunking
Electrical wiring, telephone cables and small-diameter pipework runs all lend themselves to distribution in specially designed skirting trunking. Proprietary skirting trunking systems are available in plastic or metal, and comprise compartments and dividers in which to locate small-diameter service runs. A number of different cross-sections are available, giving a wide choice of skirting profiles to suit most internal designs.

Skirting trunking fixed to perimeter walls is particularly suited to partitioned offices where the location of demountable partitions is not known at the outset, or where complete freedom is wanted to re-locate partitions from

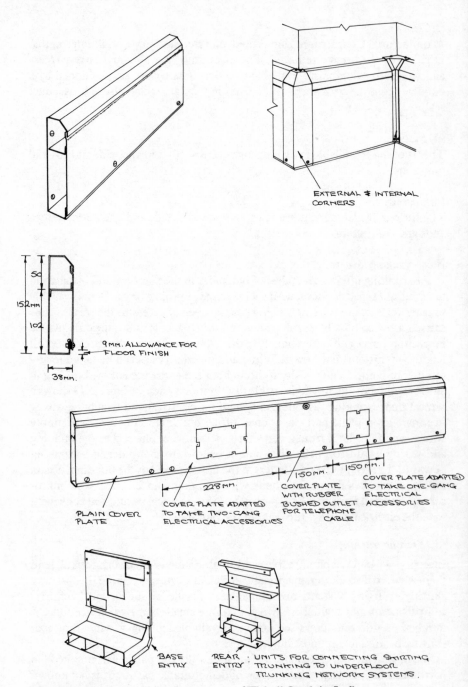

EXTERNAL & INTERNAL CORNERS

50

152MM

102

9MM. ALLOWANCE FOR FLOOR FINISH

38MM.

228 MM.

150MM.

150 MM.

PLAIN COVER PLATE

COVER PLATE ADAPTED TO TAKE TWO-GANG ELECTRICAL ACCESSORIES

COVER PLATE WITH RUBBER BUSHED OUTLET FOR TELEPHONE CABLE

COVER PLATE ADAPTED TO TAKE ONE-GANG ELECTRICAL ACCESSORIES

BASE ENTRY

REAR ENTRY

UNITS FOR CONNECTING SKIRTING TRUNKING TO UNDERFLOOR TRUNKING NETWORK SYSTEMS.

Fig. 2.12 Skirting trunking (by courtesy of Walsall Conduits Ltd)

time to time. Distribution of service runs by a combination of skirting trunking and within internal partitions is a fairly common solution in partitioned offices where hollow demountable partition systems are used. In open-plan offices, service runs can be distributed by a combination of skirting trunking and floor trunking, special connectors being used to link the two. The skirting trunking, illustrated in Fig. 2.12, is a typical fully co-ordinated system, capable of being used with compatible floor-trunking where required. The trunking is manufactured from 1.2 mm-thick zinc-coated mild steel and supplied in 2 m lengths. Accessories include straight-connectors, internal and external angles, stop-ends, cover plates to take telephone cable outlets and single or double socket outlets, and connectors for joining the skirting trunking to underfloor trunking of the same make.

(e) Horizontal service ducts

The vertical distribution of service runs, particularly in larger, more complex buildings, is normally restricted to specially constructed vertical ducts which may be either independent or form part of a service core. The use of vertical ducts and service cores will be discussed later.

The horizontal distribution of service runs from vertical ducts has a much wider range of solutions, including those previously described. Alternatively,

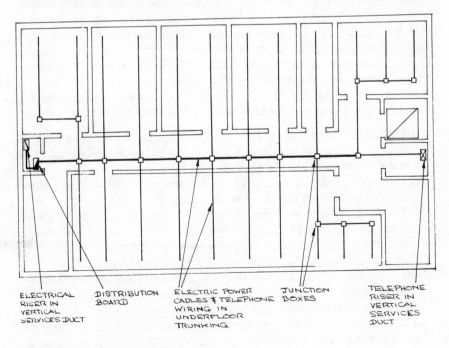

ELECTRICAL RISER IN VERTICAL SERVICES DUCT   DISTRIBUTION BOARD   ELECTRIC POWER CABLES & TELEPHONE WIRING IN UNDERFLOOR TRUNKING   JUNCTION BOXES   TELEPHONE RISER IN VERTICAL SERVICES DUCT

Fig. 2.13 Typical floor-trunking layout

where the number and nature of the service runs in a building justify it, specially constructed horizontal service ducts may be used. Horizontal service ducts used for bulky services or groups of service runs are normally storey-height and constructed from reinforced concrete, brickwork or blockwork as permanent elements of the building. Such ducts are provided with strategic access points and room for maintenance operatives to walk along them and gain easy access to the various service runs.

Service runs may be suspended from the ceiling of a service duct, fixed to its walls, or carried by an independent supporting framework within the duct. A number of proprietary services support systems are available which have been designed to convey and support service runs within service ducts and in other suitable locations. Many such proprietary services support systems, are based upon standard cold-rolled channel sections fabricated from mild steel strip. These channel sections can be cast into concrete floor slab soffits and walls, surface-fixed to concrete, brickwork or blockwork, or used to construct independent frameworks to act as the basic supports for a wide range of accessories used to carry service runs. The accessory range includes pipe clamps, hangers, rollers, cable trays and support brackets, etc., designed to provide support to piped and ducted services and cable runs. Most of the components and accessories of these systems are connected using specially grooved nuts which lock into the lipped edges of the channel sections. Figure 2.14 illustrates a typical channel section and shows how the securing nut functions. Figure 2.15 illustrates the use of channel and accessories to provide a hanging support framework for piped services from a service duct ceiling or above a suspended ceiling. A typical independent support framework for use within a service duct is illustrated in Fig. 2.16.

When considering the use of service ducts for the concealment and distribution of service runs, the following factors should be borne in mind:

(i) The use of service ducts reduces the net floor area of a building, whereas alternative means of services distribution, such as suspended ceiling voids, make no demands on floor area.

(ii) To make their use viable, a large number of service runs must be grouped together inside each horizontal service duct.

(iii) The need for such grouping of the service runs places a much greater restriction on their location than with alternative means of concealment and distribution such as within suspended ceiling voids, where service runs may be located almost anywhere over the building's area.

(iv) To provide 'walk-in' access to the service runs and ease of maintenance as well as space for the service runs themselves, service ducts must have a minimum width in the region of 1.2 – 1.5 m.

(v) Where service runs are concealed in a horizontal duct, it is unlikely that the entire length of each run will coincide with the duct, and therefore

34

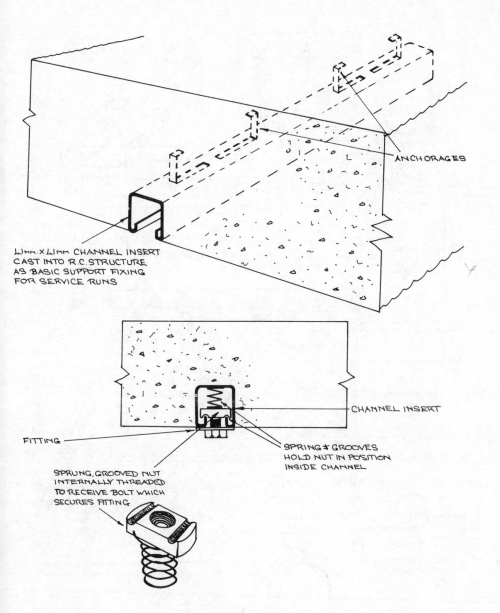

ANCHORAGES

41mm X 41mm CHANNEL INSERT
CAST INTO R.C. STRUCTURE
AS BASIC SUPPORT FIXING
FOR SERVICE RUNS

CHANNEL INSERT

FITTING

SPRING & GROOVES
HOLD NUT IN POSITION
INSIDE CHANNEL

SPRUNG, GROOVED NUT
INTERNALLY THREADED
TO RECEIVE BOLT WHICH
SECURES FITTING

Fig. 2.14 Channel and fittings services support system

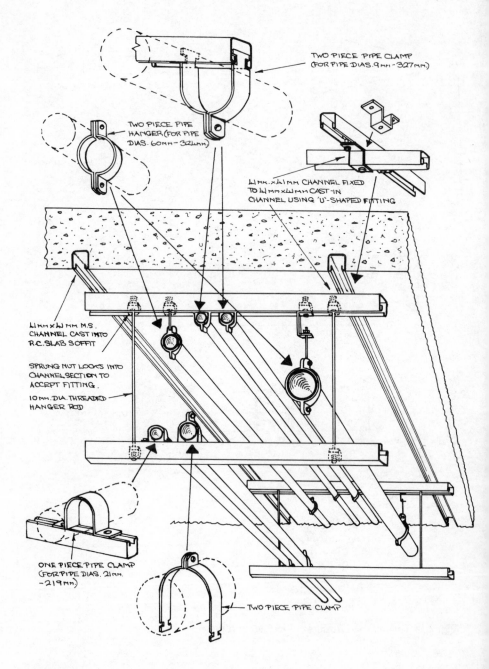

TWO PIECE PIPE CLAMP
(FOR PIPE DIAS. 9mm – 327mm)

TWO PIECE PIPE
HANGER (FOR PIPE
DIAS. 60mm – 324mm)

41mm × 41mm CHANNEL FIXED
TO 41mm × 41mm CAST-IN
CHANNEL USING 'U'-SHAPED FITTING

41mm × 41mm M.S.
CHANNEL CAST INTO
R.C. SLAB SOFFIT

SPRUNG NUT LOCKS INTO
CHANNEL SECTION TO
ACCEPT FITTING.

10mm. DIA. THREADED
HANGER ROD

ONE PIECE PIPE CLAMP
(FOR PIPE DIAS. 21mm
– 219mm)

TWO PIECE PIPE CLAMP

Fig. 2.15 Channel and fitting services support system – support framework hung from RC soffit above suspended ceiling or inside services duct

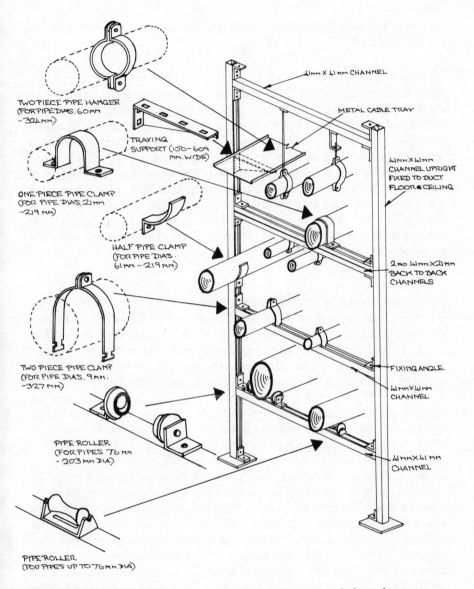

TWO PIECE PIPE HANGER
(FOR PIPE DIAS. 60mm
-324mm)

ONE PIECE PIPE CLAMP
(FOR PIPE DIAS. 21mm
-219mm)

HALF PIPE CLAMP
(FOR PIPE DIAS.
61mm – 219mm)

TWO PIECE PIPE CLAMP
(FOR PIPE DIAS. 9mm.
-327mm)

PIPE ROLLER
(FOR PIPES 76mm
- 203mm DIA)

PIPE ROLLER
(FOR PIPES UP TO 76mm DIA)

41mm X 41mm CHANNEL

METAL CABLE TRAY

TRAYING
SUPPORT (150-609
mm. WIDE)

41mm X 41mm
CHANNEL UPRIGHT
FIXED TO DUCT
FLOOR & CEILING

2 no. 41mm X 21mm
BACK TO BACK
CHANNELS

FIXING ANGLE

41mm X 41mm
CHANNEL

41mm X 41mm
CHANNEL

Fig. 2.16 Channel and fitting services support system – independent support framework inside services duct

other methods of concealment will be essential in conjunction with the services duct.

(f) Vertical ducts and service cores

With the exception of small-diameter pipework and wiring which may be capable of distribution within hollow partitions or other vertical elements, the majority of vertical service runs in larger, more complex buildings will require specially constructed vertical service ducts for their concealment and distribution. The walls of such ducts are usually constructed from reinforced concrete, brickwork or blockwork, and may be independent or form part of the building's main service core. In buildings of large plan area, independent ducts at various strategic positions, as well as ducts contained in the service core, will be necessary in order to reduce the need for excessively long horizontal service runs which would result if all of the vertical runs were confined to the service core.

(g) Service cores

Today, many building types are medium or high rise and their basic designs comprise large open-plan floor areas, capable of flexible sub-division according to the particular user's requirements. A typical example is the office building, although many other buildings, including shops, educational buildings, hospitals, etc., are designed in this way. An important factor in the layout of such buildings is the efficient access of their users to various parts of each floor, without having to travel excessive distances. In most medium- and high-rise buildings, the principal vertical link will be the lift system; because lift systems take up a large area, their size and location will have a significant effect on the overall design and floor layout.

The lift walls and associated landing space on each floor form a key element in the circulation on each floor, and the vertical shaft comprises an important structural element in the building. It is logical, therefore, to locate the stairs, toilets, cleaners' rooms, etc., in a group near to the lifts, thus facilitating easy access to them since any circulation space will clearly originate at the lifts. In addition, vertical ducts for services can be grouped together with these other elements, thereby avoiding their interference with the open plan layout of the remaining floor areas. By locating the vertical services ducts adjacent to the building's main circulation areas, easy access to the various service runs is possible for maintenance work, etc., without interfering with the main floor areas and the activities therein.

In a building of large plan area, the service core thus created can be centrally located to minimize horizontal travel distances of people using each floor. In addition, it is structurally advantageous to place this stiff element in a central position. The actual positioning of the service core will be dictated by a combination of the following factors:

(i) Means of escape in case of fire. Maximum travel distances from floor areas to escape routes are dictated by various regulations.
(ii) Firefighting requirements.
(iii) Convenience of access by the building's users to floor areas.
(iv) Structural design considerations where the service core is being used as a vertical stiffening element, or where its walls are being used as structural supports to the floors.

In buildings with large plan areas, however, where horizontal piped, ducted and wired service runs need to be widely dispersed, the grouping of all their vertical runs in a central service core may be uneconomical, requiring excessively long horizontal runs. In such cases, it will be necessary to provide independent vertical ducts at other positions in the building's plan in addition to those within the main service core.

Figure 2.17 shows a typical service core layout suitable for a multi-storey office building. The service core contains the main vertical circulation elements along with toilets, kitchens and cleaners' rooms on each floor level. The toilets, kitchens and cleaners' rooms all require hot- and cold-water supplies and waste installations; it is therefore economical to group them vertically above each other within the service core, adjacent to the services duct containing the main vertical water supply and waste services. This vertical grouping, adjacent to the water supply and waste services duct, reduces the need for long horizontal pipe runs which would be necessary if these facilities were dispersed throughout the building's plan area. Thus, in addition to being convenient for the building's users, vertical grouping of toilets, etc. within the main service core is economical in that it reduces the number of horizontal service runs required.

The service core also contains a number of other ducts carrying essential vertical service runs. These include a dry riser duct, refuse chute, air-conditioning supply and extract ducts, electrical duct and GPO riser. As previously stated, where the building concerned has a large plan area, independent vertical services ducts will be required, separate from those contained in the main service core, if excessively long, and therefore uneconomical, horizontal services runs are to be avoided. In the example shown in Fig. 2.17, additional independent vertical ducts are used for the air-conditioning supply and extract in order to reduce the amount of horizontal air-conditioning ductwork. The additional dry-riser duct is provided to increase the efficiency of the building's firefighting system.

Figure 2.18 shows the detailed layout and construction of the service core on the ground floor and upper floors. Since the service core is based upon the main vertical circulation routes within the building, its ground floor plan design must incorporate the main entrance and reception area. Note that the locations of the vertical ducts, which must run the full height of the building, are in the same positions on both the ground and upper floor plans.

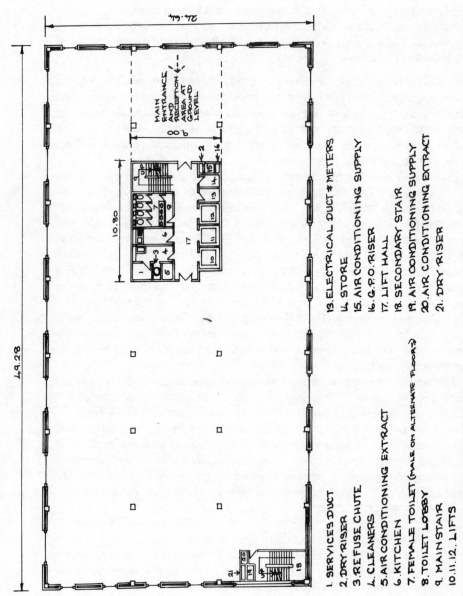

Fig. 2.17 Multi-storey office building: service core layout – general view

1. SERVICES DUCT
2. DRY RISER
3. REFUSE CHUTE
4. CLEANERS
5. AIR CONDITIONING EXTRACT
6. KITCHEN
7. FEMALE TOILET (MALE ON ALTERNATE FLOORS)
8. TOILET LOBBY
9. MAIN STAIR
10. 11. 12. LIFTS
13. ELECTRICAL DUCT & METERS
14. STORE
15. AIR CONDITIONING SUPPLY
16. G.P.O. RISER
17. LIFT HALL
18. SECONDARY STAIR
19. AIR CONDITIONING SUPPLY
20. AIR CONDITIONING EXTRACT
21. DRY RISER

MAIN ENTRANCE AND RECEPTION AREA AT GROUND LEVEL

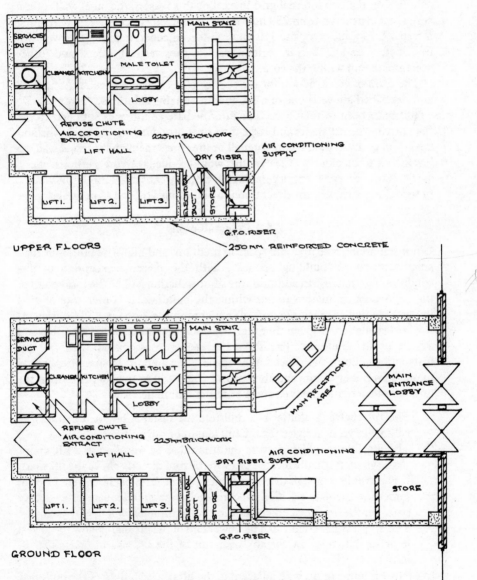

Fig. 2.18 Multi-storey office building: service core layout – details

Building Services Integration

Figure 2.17 shows that, in addition to acting as a central vertical stiffening element, the service core's main walls also provide structural support to the building's reinforced concrete floors, replacing four of the intermediate columns on the two internal grid lines. For this reason, the main walls of the core are constructed from 250 mm-thick reinforced concrete. The remaining internal core walls comprise 150 mm reinforced concrete to the stairwell and lift shafts, and 225 mm brickwork to the vertical ducts and other accommodation within the core.

The form of construction for the service core shown in Figs 2.17 and 2.18 and described above is one of a number of suitable solutions. An alternative would have been to retain the four intermediate columns as supports to the floors, trim the lift shafts and large duct openings with structural downstand beams on each floor, and construct all of the core's main and internal walls in brickwork or blockwork. Clearly, this would reduce the core's efficiency as a vertical stiffening element in comparison with the chosen solution; this would, in turn, have a significant effect upon the building's overall structural design.

2.5 Lift installations

Lift installations take up more space in medium- and high-rise buildings than any of the other building services, with the possible exception of air-conditioning systems. In addition, the lift installation will be the focal point of the main user circulation routes within the building. It is therefore of vital importance that the major factors of spatial requirements for, and location of, the lift installation be given thorough consideration in the initial planning and design of the building. The following elements associated with any lift installation require the allocation of space – the amount of space depending upon the number of lifts and their sizes, which will in turn depend upon the number of users and the type and size of the building.

(a) The lift shaft, or shafts in a multiple lift installation, requires a large volume of vertical space for the full height of the building.
(b) The machinery which powers the lifts must be installed in a lift motor room which is usually located on or in the roof directly above the lift shaft. It is possible to install drive machinery at the base of the lift shaft, or at some intermediate position, and in each case an adequate provision of space for the drive machinery and control equipment will have to be made.
(c) The lift pit is an extension of the lower end of the lift shaft below the lowest floor served, to allow for any over-run of the lift and to house the lift buffers.
(d) The lift lobby or lift hall, adjacent to the lifts on each floor of the building, for passengers to await the arrival of the lifts, and to link the vertical circulation route provided by the lifts to the horizontal circulation routes at each floor level.

Figure 2.19 shows the layout of a typical single lift installation and its vertical and horizontal space requirements within the building for lift cars of different capacities. It should be borne in mind that large buildings like the one shown in Figs 2.17 and 2.18 require multiple lift installations and the space requirements will therefore need to be increased in proportion to those shown in Fig. 2.19. A triple lift installation of the type shown in Figs 2.17 and 2.18 and its lift hall account for some 20 m^2 of floor space at each level, totalling 140 m^2 in a seven-storey building. In terms of rental value over the life of the building, this amount of space useage represents a significant loss of income and illustrates the importance of giving very detailed consideration to the extent of lift services required. One lift too many not only incurs additional capital cost, but will add to maintenance costs and reduce rental income throughout the life of the building.

It was stated at the beginning of this section that air-conditioning systems take up much space within the building. However, the principal difference between the spatial requirements of air-conditioning systems and lift installations is that the former make little demand upon useable floor space, since the plant is often located in rooftop or basement plantrooms, and the horizontal ductwork above suspended ceilings. Generally, only the vertical duct runs reduce the building's useable floor area.

The opening required through each structural floor for the lift shaft will, in most cases, be of sufficient area to require the provision of structural downstand beams to trim it, particularly in the case of a multiple lift installation. The shaft walls themselves may be constructed in reinforced concrete, brickwork or blockwork, and it is vital that they be truly vertical, smooth and free from any undesirable projections. The only permissible projection into the lift shaft will be the ledge or sill at the foot of the door opening at each landing to take the landing doors. This projecting ledge or sill may be of reinforced concrete constructed monolithically with the concrete floor slab or downstand beam, or a steel section sill bolted to the trimmed floor slab edge.

The lift motor room is, as previously stated, normally located on the roof and directly above the lift shaft. Its plan area will be larger than that of the lift shaft, but this should not present any problems, since roof level space for plant rooms is usually quite plentiful. Rooftop motor rooms are usually constructed from brickwork or blockwork, directly off a section of roof slab which must be structurally designed to carry the loads imposed by the lift cars, counter-weights, drive machinery and control equipment. Good ventilation of up to 30 air changes per hour is essential to dissipate the heat generated by the lift machinery.

The lift pit is a vertical downward continuation of the lift shaft, extending 1 to 2 m below the lowest floor level served. The lift pit provides an over-run allowance for the lift cars, and houses the buffers which are of the spring type

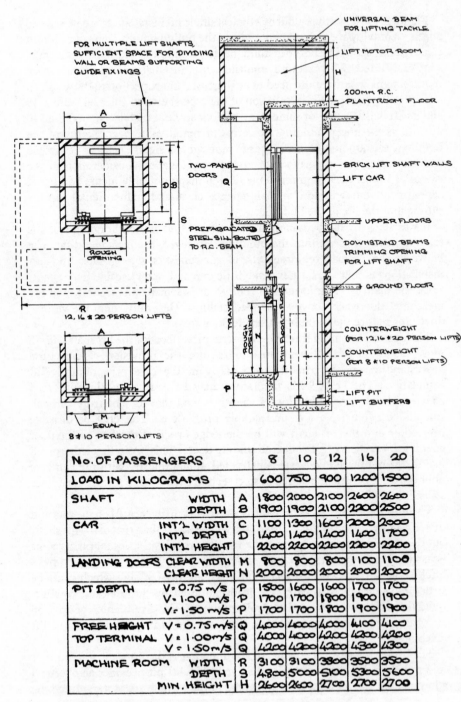

No. OF PASSENGERS			8	10	12	16	20
LOAD IN KILOGRAMS			600	750	900	1200	1500
SHAFT	WIDTH	A	1800	2000	2100	2600	2600
	DEPTH	B	1900	1900	2100	2200	2500
CAR	INT'L WIDTH	C	1100	1300	1600	2000	2000
	INT'L DEPTH	D	1400	1400	1400	1400	1700
	INT'L HEIGHT		2200	2200	2200	2200	2200
LANDING DOORS	CLEAR WIDTH	M	800	800	800	1100	1100
	CLEAR HEIGHT	N	2000	2000	2000	2000	2000
PIT DEPTH	V = 0.75 m/s	P	1500	1600	1600	1700	1700
	V = 1.00 m/s	P	1700	1700	1800	1900	1900
	V = 1.50 m/s	P	1700	1700	1800	1900	1900
FREE HEIGHT TOP TERMINAL	V = 0.75 m/s	Q	4000	4000	4000	4100	4100
	V = 1.00 m/s	Q	4000	4000	4200	4200	4200
	V = 1.50 m/s	Q	4200	4200	4200	4300	4300
MACHINE ROOM	WIDTH	R	3100	3100	3500	3500	3500
	DEPTH	S	4800	5000	5100	5300	5600
	MIN. HEIGHT	H	2600	2600	2700	2700	2700

Fig. 2.19 Passenger lift installation showing space requirements

for slower speed lifts and oil-loaded for high speed lifts. Where necessary, the lift pit should be waterproofed to prevent ingress of ground water.

2.6 Services integration and the Building Regulations

Several aspects of services integration within buildings are affected directly or indirectly by provisions contained in the Building Regulations (1976). The provisions which affect services integration most significantly are contained in Part E: *Safety in fire*, although there are other provisions which place minor constraints on services installations. In this section, Part E of the Building Regulations (1976) is dealt with in detail, followed by a short summary of the other parts of the regulations which place constraints on the integration of services.

2.6.1 The Building Regulations (1976), Part E *Safety in fire*

The nature of certain building services, and the ways in which they are integrated within buildings, can make a potentially significant contribution to the spread of fire if proper precautions are not taken in their design and installation. This is particularly so in the case of long service runs, services voids and ducts which connect several different parts of the building on their routes from plant rooms or appliances to their various outlets. Their commonality to many different zones of the building can result in 'short-circuiting' of otherwise adequate fire-resistant constructions designed to restrict fire-spread throughout the building.

Part E of the Building Regulations places significant constraints upon the integration of services within buildings and their relationship with the structure and fabric as it affects the outbreak and spread of fire.

Before considering the subsections of Part E which have a direct relevance to building services, it is necessary to appreciate one of the major principles of fire protection in buildings. The protection of buildings and their occupants in the event of fire is based upon four major principles, these being:

(a) Space separation between different buildings
(b) Internal compartmentation (or subdivision) of individual buildings
(c) Fire-resistance of elements of structure
(d) Means of escape

The principle of internal compartmentation involves the physical subdivision of a building into smaller, fire-tight zones or compartments by walls and floors of a specified fire resistance (known as compartment walls and floors) in order to restrict the spread of fire throughout the building. Thus, in a large building, a fire breaking out in a particular compartment should be contained within that compartment, by virtue of its fire-resisting boundary

45

walls and floors, for a sufficient length of time for the fire brigade to arrive and extinguish it before it penetrates to adjacent compartments and throughout the building. This containment of the fire within its 'outbreak zone' also means that persons inside that zone need only move through fire-resisting doors into an adjacent compartment in order to be in a position of relative safety before subsequently leaving the building.

The sub-division of buildings into compartments is controlled by Building Regulation E.4: *Provision of compartment walls and compartment floors*. Regulation E.4(1) requires that buildings of certain purpose-groups, whose sizes exceed certain specified limits, must be divided into compartments by means of compartment walls or compartment floors. The specific requirements are laid down in the Table to Regulation E.4. Thus, a building in Purpose Group III: *Other Residential*, which exceeds 28 m in height and whose floor areas in each storey exceed 2000 m^2, must have each storey subdivided into compartments not exceeding 2000 m^2 in area and 5500 m^3 in volume. If the height of the building does not exceed 28 m, these limits are increased to 3000 m^2 and 8500 m^3 respectively. In addition to the main compartmentation requirements covered by Regulation E.4(1) and the Table to Regulation E.4, certain other provisions affect the compartmentation of buildings and these are laid down in Regulation E.4(2) and (3).

Another important provision within Part E of the Building Regulations, which must be considered together with compartmentation, is Part E.10: *Protected shafts*. A protected shaft is defined as a stairway, lift, escalator, chute, duct or other shaft which enables persons, things or air to pass between different compartments (see Regulation E.1). It is clear, therefore, that with the exception of stairways, protected shafts are principally associated with vertical services installations. Vertical services, such as lifts, refuse chutes, ducts, etc., form a physical link between the horizontal compartments within a building, and to prevent fire spreading between compartments up or down the building via these vertical links, it is essential that they are contained within their own separate fire-tight zones. Regulation E.10 lays down strict requirements for these protected shafts and the protecting structures which enclose them; these are discussed later. Figure 2.20 illustrates the compartmentation of a typical building and the provision of protected shafts to conform with the main provisions of Regulations E.4 and E.10.

The fire-resistance of compartment walls, compartment floors and the protecting structures which form protected shafts must comply with Building Regulation E.5, and the minimum periods of fire-resistance are, for the majority of cases, laid down in the Table to Regulation E.5. Thus, for the Purpose Group III building exceeding 28 m in height which was referred to earlier, the minimum period of fire-resistance for these elements would be 1.5 h. This reduces to 1 h if the height of the building does not exceed 28 m.

It has already been stated that building services can make a potential

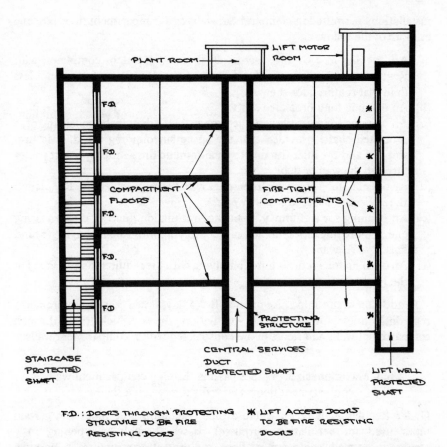

PLANT ROOM

LIFT MOTOR ROOM

F.D.

F.D.

COMPARTMENT FLOORS

FIRE-TIGHT COMPARTMENTS

F.D.

F.D.

F.D

PROTECTING STRUCTURE

STAIRCASE PROTECTED SHAFT

CENTRAL SERVICES DUCT PROTECTED SHAFT

LIFT WELL PROTECTED SHAFT

F.D. : DOORS THROUGH PROTECTING STRUCTURE TO BE FIRE RESISTING DOORS

✳ LIFT ACCESS DOORS TO BE FIRE RESISTING DOORS

Fig. 2.20 Section through building showing compartmentation and protected shafts

significant contribution to the spread of fire throughout the building. One of the main problems lies in the fact that many service-runs will almost certainly have to travel through a number of the building's compartments on their routes from plant rooms or appliances to their various outlets in other parts of the building. If proper precautions are not taken, these service runs may, by their commonality to several of the building's compartments, allow fire to spread throughout the building via the fire-resisting constructions which they penetrate. To prevent this possibility, various provisions relating specifically to services installations are laid down in Part E of the Building Regulations (1976) and are described below.

2.6.2 Perforation of compartment walls and compartment floors

Under Building Regulation E.9(1), the only openings related to services

47

installations permitted in compartment walls and compartment floors are one or more of the following:

(a) An opening in a compartment wall fitted with a door complying with Regulation E.11 (*Fire-resisting doors*) and having a fire-resistance not less than that required for the wall
(b) An opening for a protected shaft
(c) An opening for a ventilation duct (other than a duct in, or consisting of, a protected shaft) provided that the space surrounding the duct is fire-stopped and the duct fitted with an automatic fire shutter where it passes through the wall or floor
(d) An opening for a pipe which complies with the requirements of Regulation E.12 (*Penetration of structure by pipes*)
(e) An opening for a chimney, appliance ventilation duct, or duct encasing one or more flue pipes, in each case complying with Regulation E.9(5) and Part L as relevant
(f) An opening for a refuse chute complying with the requirements of Part J of the Regulations.

In addition to the above, Regulation E.9(5) lays down certain requirements regarding flues and appliance ventilation ducts which pass through compartment walls and floors or are constructed within compartment walls.

2.6.3 Maximum sizes of pipes passing through compartment walls, compartment floors and walls to protected shafts

Under Regulation E.12(2), where a pipe (excluding flue pipes and certain pipes used for ventilation purposes) passes through an opening in a compartment wall, compartment floor or a protecting structure, its nominal diameter must not exceed that listed in the Table to Regulation E.12 (see Table 2.1). In addition, the Regulation stipulates that the opening must be as small as practicable and fire-stopped around the pipe.

There are two minor exceptions to the requirements of Regulation E.12(2) which concern above ground drainage pipes in houses, flats and maisonettes. These exceptions are dealt with under Regulation E.12(3).

2.6.4 Fire-stopping around service runs passing through compartment walls, compartment floors and walls to protected shafts

Building Regulation E.14(1)(a) defines a fire-stop as a seal of non-combustible material provided to close an imperfection of fit between elements, components or construction in a building so as to restrict penetration of smoke or flame through that imperfection. Regulation E.14(10) requires that any opening, through any element of structure (which includes compartment

48

Table 2.1 Table to Regulation E.12 – Maximum nominal internal diameter of pipes

Specification of pipe	Maximum nominal internal diameter of pipe (mm)
(1)	(2)
(a) Pipe made of any non-combustible material which, if exposed to a temperature of 800 °C, will not soften and will not fracture to such an extent as to permit flames or hot gases to pass through the wall of the pipe	150
(b) Pipe made of lead or aluminium or alloy thereof; asbestos-cement pipe; or unplasticized polyvinyl chloride (PVC) pipe complying with BS 4514:1969	100 if it penetrates structure (other than a separating wall) enclosing a protected shaft not regularly used for the passage of people 38 in all other cases
(c) Pipe made of any other material	38

walls, compartment floors and walls to protected shafts) for the passage of a pipe, duct, conduit or cable, shall be no larger than is necessary and shall be fire-stopped. Fire-stopping around pipes and ducts must not restrict their thermal movements and non-rigid fire-stopping materials must be reinforced with, or supported by, non-combustible materials to prevent their displacement.

Some of the methods and materials used to provide fire-stopping around service runs where they penetrate fire resisting constructions are described below, and illustrated in Fig. 2.21.

(a) Intumescent fire sleeves

Intumescent material, in strip or sheet form, has the appearance of ordinary plastic sheet but, on exposure to fire, the material foams up and swells to several times its original thickness. A proprietary fitting, designed to act as fire-stopping around pipes, comprises a sleeve or collar made up of multiple intumescent sheets which is clamped around pipes at points where fire-stopping is required. The advantage of the intumescent fire-sleeve is that its layers are sufficiently flexible to allow any thermal or other movements to occur in the pipe but, on exposure to fire, the layers swell up, completely sealing off any gaps around the pipe. Intumescent fire-sleeves are particularly useful for PVC pipes since their swelling is capable of crushing and closing off the pipe, thereby preventing its interior bore from acting as a flue and transmitting smoke and flames through the fire-resisting element.

49

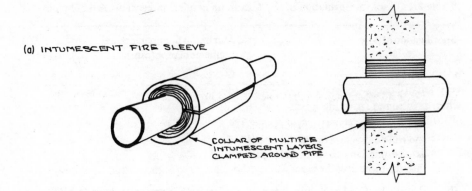

(a) INTUMESCENT FIRE SLEEVE

COLLAR OF MULTIPLE
INTUMESCENT LAYERS
CLAMPED AROUND PIPE

(b) MINERAL WOOL FIRE PILLOWS

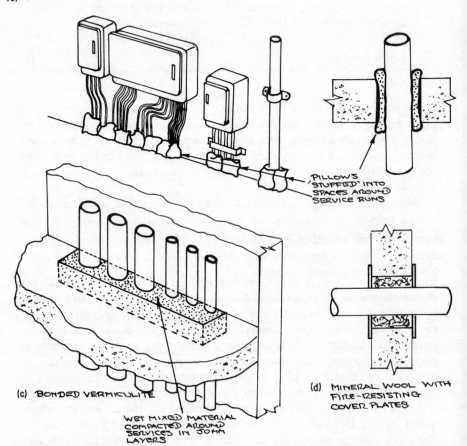

PILLOWS
STUFFED INTO
SPACES AROUND
SERVICE RUNS

(c) BONDED VERMICULITE

WET MIXED MATERIAL
COMPACTED AROUND
SERVICES IN 50MM
LAYERS

(d) MINERAL WOOL WITH
FIRE-RESISTING
COVER PLATES

Fig. 2.21 Fire-stopping

(b) Mineral wool fire pillows

Proprietary fire pillows, 300 mm square × 38 mm thick, made of fire-resistant cloth and filled with mineral wool are compressed and 'stuffed' into openings around conduits, pipes, cables, wires and ducting where they pass through fire-resisting constructions. The pillows are capable of being compressed into very small spaces between service runs and the surrounding structure and, when positioned, provide a fire-resistance of 3 h. The compressibility of fire pillows allows thermal and other movements to take place in the service runs where necessary, and a further advantage is their ability to be removed easily for maintenance or alteration of the service runs concerned.

Fire pillows are not generally suitable for fire-stopping around services which are visible to building users since, as shown in Fig. 2.21, a neat, aesthetically acceptable finish cannot be readily achieved.

(c) Bonded vermiculite

Bonded vermiculite is a proprietary wet-applied fire-stopping material comprising exfoliated vermiculite mixed with a specially formulated fire-resistant bonding fluid. Vermiculite is a naturally occurring mineral which, when subjected to heat treatment, exfoliates, resulting in a material with superior fire-resisting properties. The two materials are mixed in the proportions 28.4 litres of vermiculite to 2.5 litres of bonding fluid; the resulting material is applied where required in accordance with the manufacturer's instructions. Immediately before filling the space which requires fire-stopping, a coat of the bonding fluid is brushed on all contact surfaces. The bonded vermiculite mixture is then placed in layers of approximately 50 mm thick, each layer being tamped and carefully compacted around the service runs to be fire-stopped. This procedure is repeated until the required thickness is achieved. In most cases, temporary formwork will be required for the installation of bonded vermiculite fire-stopping and it is necessary to line the formwork with thin polythene in order to facilitate its striking after the material has set.

(d) Mineral wool with fire-resisting cover plates

An effective method of fire-stopping is to pack mineral wool into the space around the service run and to fix fire-resistant cover plates on both faces to retain the mineral wool in position and to provide a neat finish. This method is particularly suitable where the gap to be fire-stopped is large (between 13 and 60 mm) and where a large amount of thermal movement must be accommodated due to the nature of the service run being treated.

(e) Gypsum plaster or cement mortar

For fire-stopping small gaps (up to 13 mm), for example around pipes, gypsum plaster or cement mortar may be suitable. Gypsum plaster is preferable since it

Building Services Integration

undergoes less shrinkage on setting and has superior fire-resistance. Shrinkage creates a greater problem where cement-based products are used and to prevent shrinkage cracks, which may allow fire and smoke to penetrate, an expansion agent should be used. It should be borne in mind that neither of these materials is suitable where thermal movement of the service run is expected, since they both provide a rigid surround which would resist such movement.

2.6.5 Prevention of fire-spread within suspended ceiling voids

Building Regulation E.14: *Provision and construction of cavity barriers and fire-stops* was introduced into the Building Regulations (1976) with the aim of restricting the unseen spread of fire within the numerous hidden voids and cavities within buildings. Because this spread of fire is concealed, it presents a more serious danger than many other means of fire-spread; one of the greatest risks is created by the large voids formed by the widespread use of suspended ceiling systems. Suspended ceilings, which are one of the most convenient means of concealing building services, form hidden voids over very large areas; there have been numerous cases where buildings have been completely gutted because fire has been able to spread throughout the whole building area within such voids before being detected. One of the main purposes of Regulation E.14 is to ensure that the many voids found within buildings are subdivided by fire-resistant materials in order to prevent the undetected spread of fire throughout large areas. These subdivisions are known as 'cavity barriers' and are defined as constructions *provided to close a cavity against penetration of smoke or flame or provided within a cavity to restrict movement of smoke or flame within the cavity* (see Regulation E.14(1)(a)).

Regulation E.14(4) requires that, subject to certain exceptions, every cavity shall be sub-divided by means of cavity barriers in such positions that the distance between cavity barriers does not exceed the distance specified in the Table to Regulation E.14(4), as listed in Table 2.2.

Regulations E.14(8) and E.14(9) lay down more specific requirements for the construction and fire-resistance of cavity barriers. E.14(8) requires that where a cavity barrier is of such dimensions as to include within its surface a square having sides of 1 m in length, it must have a fire-resistance of not less than half an hour. Where a cavity barrier does not include within its surface a 1 m square, its construction must comply with specifications laid down by Regulation E.14(8)(b)(i)–(vi). Acceptable constructions include plasterboard not less than 12.5 mm thick, or timber not less than 38 mm thick. Regulation E.14(9) requires that cavity barriers shall be fixed in such a manner that their performance is unlikely to be adversely affected by movement of the building due to subsidence, shrinkage or thermal change, or by failure in a fire of fixings or materials against which cavity barriers abut. In addition, cavity barriers

Table 2.2   Table to Regulation E.14 – Maximum distance between cavity barriers

Location of cavity	Purpose group of building or compartment	Class of surface exposed within the cavity, excluding the surface of any pipe, cable or conduit	Maximum distance
(1)	(2)	(3)	(4)
Between a roof and a ceiling	Purpose group I and flats or maisonettes within purpose group III	Any	No limit
	Purpose group II and III except flats and maisonettes	Any	15 m and, in addition, area limited to 100 m²
	Any other purpose group	Any	20 m
Other than between a roof and a ceiling	Any purpose group	Class 0	20 m
		Other than Class 0	8 m

must be fitted tightly to rigid construction or otherwise fire-stopped at junctions with the surrounding construction. E.14(9) also requires that cavity barriers shall be imperforate with the exception of one or more permissible perforations, including pipes and ducts, listed under E.14(9)(c)(i)–(vi).

Figure 2.22 shows some typical details of cavity barriers in suspended ceiling voids which comply with the requirements of the Building Regulations.

2.6.6 Protected shafts

With the principal exception of staircases, the main purpose of protected shafts within buildings is to house vertical services. Lift shafts, refuse chutes and ducts for air-conditioning, electrical or piped services will inevitably be common to a number of compartments, particularly in tall buildings. If these vertical services were not properly enclosed by fire-resisting protecting structures, they would constitute an easy means for fire to spread between the horizontal compartments and throughout the building. In order to prevent this, Building Regulation E.10 lays down a number of requirements specifically related to protected shafts.

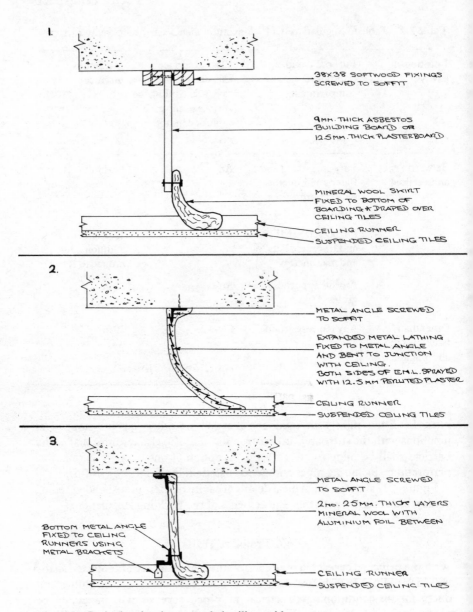

1.

38×38 SOFTWOOD FIXINGS
SCREWED TO SOFFIT

9mm. THICK ASBESTOS
BUILDING BOARD OR
12.5mm. THICK PLASTERBOARD

MINERAL WOOL SKIRT
FIXED TO BOTTOM OF
BOARDING & DRAPED OVER
CEILING TILES

CEILING RUNNER

SUSPENDED CEILING TILES

2.

METAL ANGLE SCREWED
TO SOFFIT

EXPANDED METAL LATHING
FIXED TO METAL ANGLE
AND BENT TO JUNCTION
WITH CEILING.
BOTH SIDES OF E.M.L. SPRAYED
WITH 12.5 mm PERLITED PLASTER

CEILING RUNNER

SUSPENDED CEILING TILES

3.

METAL ANGLE SCREWED
TO SOFFIT

2 no. 25mm. THICK LAYERS
MINERAL WOOL WITH
ALUMINIUM FOIL BETWEEN

BOTTOM METAL ANGLE
FIXED TO CEILING
RUNNERS USING
METAL BRACKETS

CEILING RUNNER

SUSPENDED CEILING TILES

Fig. 2.22 Cavity barriers in suspended ceiling voids

Regulation E.10(4) imposes requirements regarding the non-combustibility of protecting structures and associated elements.

Regulation E.10(6) states that there shall be no opening in any protecting structure other than any one or more of the following:

(a) An opening for a pipe complying with the requirements of Regulation E.12
(b) An opening fitted with a fire-resisting door complying with Regulation E.10(7) and with Regulation E.11 (*Fire-resisting doors*)
(c) If the protected shaft contains a lift; an opening complying with Regulation E.10(8)
(d) If the protected shaft serves as, or contains, a ventilating duct; an inlet to, or outlet from that duct or an opening for that duct.

Regulation E.10(7) lays down requirements as to the fire-resistance of doors in openings in protecting structures. In buildings of purpose group III, IV or VII, half-hour fire-resisting doors are required. In other cases, their fire-resistance must be not less than half that of the protecting structure, or half an hour, whichever is the greater.

Regulation E.10(8) requires that protected shafts containing lifts must:

(a) Be ventilated to the external air by one or more permanent openings at the top of the shaft of total unobstructed area at least 0.1 m^2 per lift and
(b) Not contain any gas or oil pipe, or ventilating duct.

The protecting structure may have an opening for the passage of lift cables into the lift motor room provided that, if the opening is at the bottom of the shaft, it shall be as small as practicable.

Regulation E.10(9) requires that, where a protected shaft contains a ventilating duct or is itself a ventilating duct, the duct must have automatic fire shutters fitted internally to reduce the risk of fire-spread from one compartment to another; also it must not be built or lined with any material which might substantially increase the risk of such fire-spread. In addition, where a protected shaft contains a ventilating duct, additional fire barriers must be provided between the duct and the shaft, as may be necessary to reduce the risk of fire-spread between compartments.

Regulation E.10(10) requires that a protected shaft containing a stairway shall not contain any pipe conveying gas or oil or any ventilating duct.

Regulation E.10(11) requires that, where a protected shaft contains a pipe conveying gas, the shaft must be adequately ventilated direct to the external air.

In addition to the Building Regulations Part E, there are certain other regulations, standards and codes which affect the integration of services with regard to fire safety; these are dealt with separately in Section 2.7.

Building Services Integration

2.6.7 Other Building Regulations provisions affecting services integration

A relatively small number of additional constraints on the integration of services are imposed by certain other parts of the Building Regulations (1976), and it is essential that they are also complied with in addition to the more extensive requirements of Part E which have previously been described. There follows a short summary of the relevant provisions and cross-reference should be made to the Building Regulations in order to understand the specific requirements.

Part G: Sound insulation of walls

Requirements regarding the construction of walls separating refuse chutes from habitable rooms and other parts of dwellings – G.1(2) and (3).

Part J: Refuse disposal

Requirements regarding the construction of refuse chutes and refuse storage container chambers.

Part K: Height of habitable rooms

Requirements regarding minimum height of habitable rooms – K.8. For a given storey height, this regulation will affect the possible depth of the suspended ceiling void available for services integration (see Section 2.4.2).

Part L: Chimneys, flue pipes, hearths and fireplace recesses

Requirements regarding construction and integration of flues.

Part M: Heat-producing appliances and incinerators

Requirements regarding flues and vents.

Part N: Drainage, private sewers and cesspools

Requirements regarding construction and accessibility of soil pipes, waste pipes and ventilating pipes – N.4. Requirements regarding placing of soil pipes and waste pipes – N.5(2).

2.7 Other regulations, standards and codes relating to fire safety

Although the most comprehensive requirements regarding fire safety associated with services installations are laid down by the Building Regulations (1976), certain other regulations, standards and codes impose constraints aimed at minimizing fire risk. These are numerous and they contain a wide range of requirements and recommendations as to good practice, many of which are not included in the Building Regulations. Some of the more important provisions are listed below:

(a) Pipes hotter than 100 °C should be separated from wood and other combustible parts of the building by an air-space of at least 50 mm. Pipes hotter than 150 °C should, in addition, be insulated with non-combustible materials (Fire Protection Association guide to safety with piped services.)

(b) Electrical services should not be installed in air ducts (BS Code of Practice 413: 1973 *Ducts for building services*).

(c) Piped services, e.g. for gas and water, should not be in close proximity to electrical services unless these services are electrically bonded to the earth of the electrical installation (*IEE Regulations for the Electrical Equipment of Buildings*, 14th ed., 1966).

(d) Combustible insulation, e.g. foam plastic, around other services should not be allowed in the same duct or close to electrical services.

(e) Services containing flammable liquids and gases should be of sufficient strength to withstand damage and should be correctly jointed. If such services are installed in a duct, no other service should be installed in the same duct and the duct should be ventilated top and bottom.

(f) Services containing flammable liquids should not be installed:

 (i) Where they are liable to be damaged (FPA guide to safety with piped services)
 (ii) In shafts containing stairs or lifts
 (iii) Close to hot plant and pipes.

(g) If a flammable liquid pipe must be run close to a hot pipe, the flammable liquid pipe should be below the hot pipe.

(h) Where pipes containing water or other liquids must run close to electrical services, the former must be positioned below the electrical services.

(i) Waste disposal chutes and associated hoppers should be completely enclosed by fire-resisting construction. Waste disposal openings should be fitted with self-closing fire-resisting flaps (BS Code of Practice 306: 1960 'The storage and on-site treatment of refuse from buildings').

(j) Pipes, fittings and jointing materials for flammable gas or compressed air should not be made from materials which may be easily melted or damaged by fire. These services should not be routed through hazardous areas such as boiler rooms, where possible.

(k) Valves for the services described above should be conveniently sited so that supplies can be cut off in emergencies (Gas Safety Regulations (1972) and FPA guide to safety with piped services).

Building Services Integration

2.8 Builders' work

Long service runs which are common to different parts of a building will inevitably have to penetrate walls, floors and other elements at some points and this requires the formation of holes of varying size and shape through these elements. The way a service hole is formed will depend upon a number of factors, including its shape, its size, the thickness of the element through which it passes, and the composition of the element. The majority of walls in large-scale buildings are constructed from brickwork, blockwork or reinforced concrete, and the floors are usually of pre-cast or in-situ reinforced concrete.

Some of the more common methods of forming services holes through walls and floors constructed from these materials are described below.

2.8.1 Walls: brickwork and blockwork

Small and medium-sized holes through brick and block walls are relatively easy to form merely by leaving out one or more units. Where larger holes are required, it will be necessary to insert a lintel at the top to support the masonry above. Clearly, any hole formed through a brick or block wall will normally be square or rectangular, and this can create problems with service runs of circular cross-section. The large gaps between, for example, a pipe and the sides of the hole through which it passes will be more difficult to fire-stop than if the hole was a circular one of slightly larger diameter than the pipe.

2.8.2 Walls: in-situ concrete

The nature of in-situ concrete allows holes of any shape to be formed through elements constructed from the material. Large holes through walls are usually formed using specially constructed timber boxes suitably braced or strutted to take the weight of the wet concrete above. The timber box is secured in the correct position with screws or nails inserted from the outside of the main shutters. The screws or nails, whose heads have been left proud, are extracted prior to the striking of the wall formwork, so that the box is left cast into the wall. Finally, the box is levered out from the wall to leave the service hole. Clearly, with large holes it will be necessary to design the reinforcement so that it does not conflict with the hole, and where the hole is wide, extra reinforcement may be required over the top to act as a supporting 'lintel'. Figure 2.23 illustrates the timber-box method of forming large holes.

Smaller holes through walls may be formed by a number of different methods, as illustrated in Fig. 2.24. Materials used to form small and medium holes include solid timber, spiral-wound cardboard tubing, steel tubing and polystyrene.

58

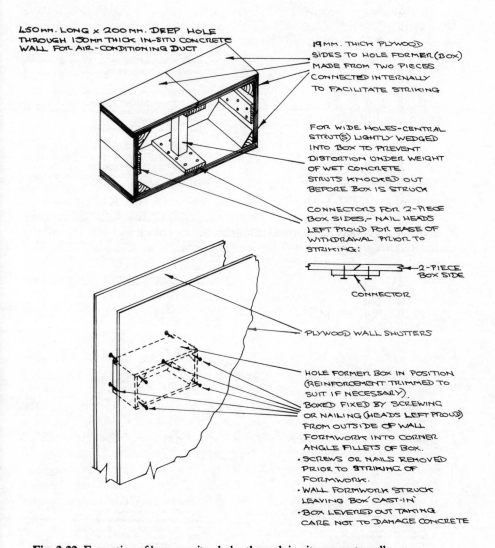

450mm. LONG x 200mm. DEEP HOLE
THROUGH 150mm THICK IN-SITU CONCRETE
WALL FOR AIR-CONDITIONING DUCT

19mm. THICK PLYWOOD
SIDES TO HOLE FORMER (BOX)
MADE FROM TWO PIECES
CONNECTED INTERNALLY
TO FACILITATE STRIKING

FOR WIDE HOLES-CENTRAL
STRUT(S) LIGHTLY WEDGED
INTO BOX TO PREVENT
DISTORTION UNDER WEIGHT
OF WET CONCRETE.
STRUTS KNOCKED OUT
BEFORE BOX IS STRUCK

CONNECTORS FOR 2-PIECE
BOX SIDES.- NAIL HEADS
LEFT PROUD FOR EASE OF
WITHDRAWAL PRIOR TO
STRIKING:

2-PIECE
BOX SIDE

CONNECTOR

PLYWOOD WALL SHUTTERS

HOLE FORMER BOX IN POSITION
(REINFORCEMENT TRIMMED TO
SUIT IF NECESSARY).
BOXED FIXED BY SCREWING
OR NAILING (HEADS LEFT PROUD)
FROM OUTSIDE OF WALL
FORMWORK INTO CORNER
ANGLE FILLETS OF BOX.
• SCREWS OR NAILS REMOVED
PRIOR TO STRIKING OF
FORMWORK.
• WALL FORMWORK STRUCK
LEAVING BOX 'CAST-IN'
• BOX LEVERED OUT TAKING
CARE NOT TO DAMAGE CONCRETE

Fig. 2.23 Formation of large services holes through in-situ concrete walls

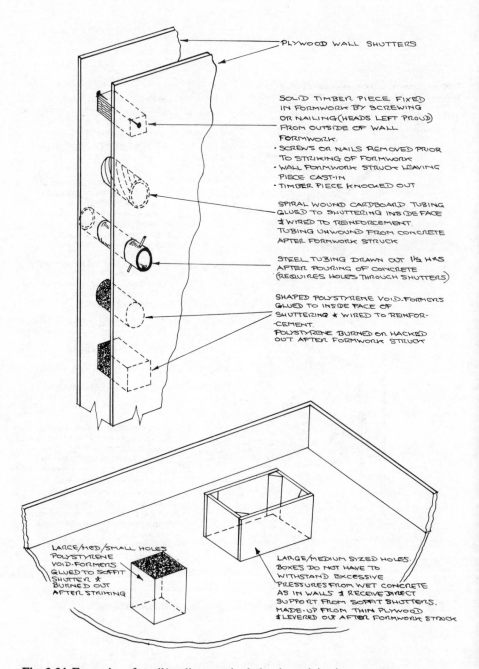

PLYWOOD WALL SHUTTERS

SOLID TIMBER PIECE FIXED
IN FORMWORK BY SCREWING
OR NAILING (HEADS LEFT PROUD)
FROM OUTSIDE OF WALL
FORMWORK.
· SCREWS OR NAILS REMOVED PRIOR
TO STRIKING OF FORMWORK
· WALL FORMWORK STRUCK LEAVING
PIECE CAST-IN
· TIMBER PIECE KNOCKED OUT

SPIRAL WOUND CARDBOARD TUBING
GLUED TO SHUTTERING INSIDE FACE
± WIRED TO REINFORCEMENT.
TUBING UNWOUND FROM CONCRETE
AFTER FORMWORK STRUCK

STEEL TUBING DRAWN OUT 1½ HRS
AFTER POURING OF CONCRETE
(REQUIRES HOLES THROUGH SHUTTERS)

SHAPED POLYSTYRENE VOID-FORMERS
GLUED TO INSIDE FACE OF
SHUTTERING ± WIRED TO REINFOR-
-CEMENT.
POLYSTYRENE BURNED OR HACKED
OUT AFTER FORMWORK STRUCK

LARGE/MED/SMALL HOLES
POLYSTYRENE
VOID-FORMERS
GLUED TO SOFFIT
SHUTTER ±
BURNED OUT
AFTER STRIKING

LARGE/MEDIUM SIZED HOLES.
BOXES DO NOT HAVE TO
WITHSTAND EXCESSIVE
PRESSURES FROM WET CONCRETE
AS IN WALLS ± RECEIVE DIRECT
SUPPORT FROM SOFFIT SHUTTERS.
MADE-UP FROM THIN PLYWOOD
± LEVERED OUT AFTER FORMWORK STRUCK

Fig. 2.24 Formation of small/medium service holes through in-situ concrete

2.8.3 Floors: in-situ concrete

The formation of holes through in-situ concrete floors is not as technically difficult as forming them through walls. The hole former does not have to support the weight of wet concrete, only a slight lateral pressure on its sides, and it is fully supported from beneath by the soffit formwork on which it stands. Very large holes, such as those required for lift wells, may have to be trimmed with downstand beams and, as with walls, all large holes will require reinforcement to be designed to avoid them.

Large to medium square or rectangular holes are usually formed using pre-made boxes of thin plywood.

For circular or other shaped holes, polystyrene void formers of a suitable cross-section may be used and burned or hacked out after the soffit forms have been struck.

Figure 2.24 illustrates typical methods for forming services holes through in-situ concrete floor slabs.

2.8.4 Floors: pre-cast concrete

Very large holes are usually formed by trimming with secondary beams linked into the main structural frame. For large and medium holes, purpose made pre-cast floor trimmers produced by the pre-cast flooring manufacturers are used.

Smaller holes of various cross-sections are usually cast into the pre-cast floor units during manufacture, but it should be noted that this requires accurate information regarding hole locations and sizes to be notified to the manufacturer well in advance of production.

2.9 Summary

The issues raised in this chapter have been essentially technical. However, they have served to illustrate the interdependence of the operations involving building work and engineering services work. In order to ensure that this interdependence is translated into reality, management has to assimilate several different items of information from different sources, probably presented in different formats. Nowadays, computers can be of assistance in this, although they require the appropriate organization structure and managerial procedures in which to operate. These aspects will be discussed in the next three chapters.

3 · Organization

3.1 Organizing for construction

We live in an *organized* society, relying on organizations to satisfy most of our needs. Modern organizations make use of formal, contractual relationships to bring together people with different but complementary skills, who collaborate in making things and providing services. In the case of building, people often come together as strangers and co-operate in the design and construction of a building.

Managers in the construction industry have the task of creating project organizations which will prove successful against whatever criteria are chosen and whatever circumstances operate. These project organizations are not always successful – in financial, technical or human terms. Sometimes they are partially successful. Managers are constantly searching for ways of designing these organizations better.

The reasons why things do not always work out well are becoming clearer. Building projects and the parent organizations which serve them have grown in scale and complexity to the point where some of them have started to become 'unmanageable'. But this is only part of the problem.

Many organizations in construction have been built on guidelines evolved decades ago in quite a different milieu. A firm founded in the twenties or thirties may still retain administrative structures and procedures which worked well at the time but are now largely inappropriate.

To improve the performance of project organizations, managers need to sharpen up their understanding of why systems fail and what can be done to design and run them better. One conclusion they may reach is that their organizations need to be *simplified* to make them more manageable. One way to do this is to decentralize some of the authority and decision-taking, so that the organization is effectively broken down into smaller, autonomous units.

However, this is not always possible or desirable. The construction of a power station, chemical plant or hospital demands the setting up of a substantial project organization, embracing a wide spectrum of technical resources and specialized skills. The manager should not ignore the possibility of simplifying such an organization, but the scope will be limited. In such cases, other ways of improving efficiency must be sought.

62

3.2 Designing an effective organization

When a client decides to build, the building industry is faced with the task of creating a *temporary* project *task-force* which can meet the client's needs and then be disbanded. Managers need to know what kind of task-force will work best. How should the overall task be broken down? How should operations be planned and monitored? How can the various inputs be integrated?

Some of the earliest attempts to answer such questions came from managers who, in the early 1900s, were struggling to cope with the relatively new problems of large-scale industrial production. These managers, whose ideas have since been labelled the *classical* approach, tried to define rules or principles for structuring an efficient organization, an example of which was the principle of the *span of control*. This stated that a manager should have no more than five or six subordinates whose work interlocks.

Such principles have been useful in providing some rule-of-thumb guidelines for setting up project organizations, but they are often too rigid. In building, a manager's span of control may vary considerably, depending on:

(a) The type of project, its component tasks and how complex they are
(b) The abilities of the manager and subordinates and the willingness of the subordinates to accept responsibility
(c) Whether or not the manager and subordinates work in close proximity
(d) The amount of time the manager spends with the group, which in turn depends on what other duties he has to perform.

In construction, many managers and their staff work away from the parent organization for a large part of the time, so that spans of control may be restricted compared with those encountered in manufacturing industries, where there is a permanent production place.

Similar arguments have limited the value of other classical guidelines for designing and running organizations; critics have pointed out that too little attention was paid both to *people* in the business and their needs and aspirations, and to the *external pressures* on the organization.

Social scientists began to offer alternative explanations of what makes an organization work well and their views have since been labelled the *human relations* approach. Their argument is that people have a big impact on the organization and that managers must recognize the importance of informal, group processes which operate through the *social* rather than organizational structure of the enterprise.

Workers' attitudes, their needs and expectations, how they feel about one another and their bosses, and the opportunities given to them, can all have a profound effect on the survival and success of the organizations involved in a building project.

People often bypass the rules and procedures of the formal system and, importantly, may further the objectives of the business more effectively by doing so. But there is a danger that the informal and formal aspects of the organization may conflict. The research findings of the social scientist have helped the manager to understand why his apparently logical plans are sometimes thwarted. But there is still a lot we do not know about human behaviour at work. For instance, it was thought that higher morale or job satisfaction would lead to higher productivity. It has proved almost impossible to produce evidence to support this belief [1].

Some managers have turned to *systems analysis* for solutions to their problems. The approach looked promising, for it brought together the classical concern for the formal, task-centred elements of organizations and the social scientists' interest in the informal, people aspects of the business. Systems thinking can contribute to the manager's understanding of the organization by showing the importance of the relationships between tasks and people and by stressing the 'openness' of the organization to outside constraints and demands. But systems analysis has so far provided comparatively little help in solving the manager's problems, probably because construction projects are highly complex and the variables – especially the human ones – are not fully understood and are not therefore entirely predictable.

Systems thinking has emphasized the similarities between project task-forces and has shown why organizations often face the same basic problems. However, the last twenty years or so has produced a mass of information to support the idea that organizations also vary a great deal in design and operation and that this has a lot to do with their *size*, type of *work*, the *people* in them and the external *market* and *economic* forces.

Joan Woodward's pioneering study of British firms was one of the first of many recent investigations which have shown that there are important differences in the way that various kinds of technology are organized [2]. Businesses like construction, producing one-off products or small batches, tend to have shallower management structures, fewer specialists and less formal rules and procedures. With fewer levels in the organization, senior managers are closer to the workface and labour relations tend to be better. The lack of formality in the task-force organization gives individuals more opportunity to negotiate their own roles and exercise initiative. In other words, they enjoy more flexibility and this makes the organizations more adaptable.

In mass-production and processing industries, Woodward found that there are more managers, more levels in the organization structure and greater administrative controls. The top managers tend to be more isolated from the workforce and industrial relations are sometimes strained.

Woodward highlighted the fact that many of the so-called principles of organization of the classical school were derived from experience of large batch or mass production operations. They may not apply to the technology of building or to the task-force demands of the project.

Burns and Stalker also looked at UK firms and found two basic approaches to organization, one more rigid than the other [3]. The more rigid approach seems to work best when the organization operates in fairly stable conditions, where technology and market pressures are not shifting too rapidly. A more flexible kind of organization seems more effective in unstable conditions, where technology is changing fast and market pressures are unpredictable.

Both kinds of organization work well providing they are matched with the technology and market forces involved. They represent the extremes of a continuum along which most organizations can be placed.

Many might argue that the building industry does not have to cope with rapid technical changes, but few would deny that effective demand for buildings is changeable and uncertain. In this respect, the industry is better served by more flexible forms of organization.

A study of the organizational problems of building firms was carried out by researchers at the Ashridge Management College. They concluded that, for *general contractors*, each new project poses fresh problems, making programming difficult and creating a need for flexibility. Co-ordination and teamwork are vital.

However, they suggested that *specialist contractors* may need a different approach to organization. Here, contracts often follow a similar pattern making programming easier. Managers tend to exercise tighter control [4].

All these results add weight to the argument that there is no 'best way' of organizing a building firm or a building project. Managers need to look at each organization on its merits, taking into account many variables. A task-force organization, as used in the construction of buildings, must be tailored to the needs of the situation. Managers must examine *what* they are trying to achieve and *how* best to compromise between conflicting requirements of the situation.

3.3 Deciding objectives

The objectives or goals of those contributing to a building project are not always readily apparent. Yet managers must identify these objectives so that they can choose criteria for judging whether the purpose of the project is being achieved. Traditionally, *profit* has been the major criterion for judging business performance, although it has come under attack from time to time. Changing attitudes have meant that profit has gradually assumed a less dominant role in management thinking and is now viewed within the context of other objectives.

The modern view is that an organization is a coalition of people. An organization cannot have objectives, only the people in it can. The goals of a business which are sometimes labelled *organizational objectives* are really those specified by the more influential, or powerful, people in it. Increasingly, these

65

objectives are being questioned both by other groups within the organization and from outside. For instance, unions and government exert pressure on the powerful members of the organization and the latter often have to modify their objectives, either to comply with statutory demands or to ensure the continued co-operation of the workforce.

Many 'organizational objectives' are not objectives at all. They are merely the *means* by which underlying goals are achieved. Profit is not a goal, it is a means of ensuring that organizations survive, that wages can be paid, that shareholders can be rewarded and, perhaps, that egos are satisfied!

To the extent that any goal can truly be said to be an organizational objective, *survival* is probably the only one. The survival of an organization affects owners, employees and their families, shareholders and community alike. Profitable projects may be a prerequisite for survival and, in this sense, profit is important as a criterion for measuring how well the organization is performing.

The purpose of setting up project organizations is to build buildings. Constructing buildings can be thought of as a *strategy* for achieving a variety of objectives for the people involved. The collective objectives of these people are assumed to be best served by completing the project on time, and at the right cost and quality. Broadly, this is true, but many of the short-term goals of the project team may conflict.

Nevertheless, managers adopt criteria of *time, quality* and *cost* to measure the performance of the project task-force. These criteria are quantifiable and are therefore useful to the manager. There are fixed dates for starting and finishing operations, agreed rates for operational tasks, and written specifications of materials and workmanship.

But there are other 'hidden' objectives which are all too often ignored. One is that the project should provide meaningful work for the people who take part in it – work which gives them comradeship, recognition and a sense of achievement and satisfaction. The enlightened manager tries to reach a compromise between the economic and human goals of the project.

From the viewpoint of the parent companies, objectives may change and new strategies may be developed. But, at the project level, the goals are fairly static and well understood by those involved. This does not mean that they are easily achieved. Managers must pay a lot of attention to the design of the project organization if it is to be successful. Systems must be created for obtaining feedback on project performance. The feedback must be compared with targets. Unless suitable procedures are developed and communication links formed, the success of the project cannot be measured and shortcomings cannot be rectified.

3.4 Project structure

It is generally accepted that the building project requires a hierarchical structure of activities. In the broadest terms, the hierarchy can be split into a *decision* level and an *action* level. But to understand the design of an effective task-force, it is worthwhile developing this distinction.

One approach is to split the activities of the project team into four groups:

(a) *Deciding policy*: The task force must have a sense of direction, priorities must be worked out and standards established. Overall guidance must be given by the parent organizations.
(b) *Developing new ideas*: The organizations involved in the project will be constantly adapting what they do and how they do it, to cope with competition and other external and internal pressures and constraints.
(c) *Maintaining the steady state*: All the routine operations which contribute to, or support, the production of the building must be organized and co-ordinated.
(d) *Coping with breakdowns and crises*: Things will go wrong. There must be a mechanism for dealing with the unexpected.

Deciding policy and developing new ideas are largely the province of the parent organizations involved in the project. Members of the task-force will be primarily concerned with maintaining the steady state – getting the job built on time and within budget – and coping with operational breakdowns and problems.

Another analysis of organizational activity visualizes three levels of action [5]. Figure 3.1 illustrates this approach.

(a) Strategic

The part of the organization which decides where it is going and sets standards by which its progress can be measured. Senior management are most obviously involved in this work and they have to rely heavily on experience, judgement and often hunch. They check that the organization remains attuned to environmental constraints, aims at the right markets, produces the right products and is prepared for trends and events. They cope with uncertainty and risk, having little or no control over some of the events which affect the building industry and its member firms.

(b) Technical

The part of the organization concerned with the production work and sometimes called the operational level. This is the 'doing' level of the organization, where the product is made or the service rendered. Managers and staff at this level are concerned with day-to-day production problems. Their concern is primarily with the efficient use of resources, their timescale is short-term and their decisions rely on facts. They are protected from some of the uncertainties that affect the business, because these are dealt with by senior managers. Much of the work of the project task-force is at this technical level.

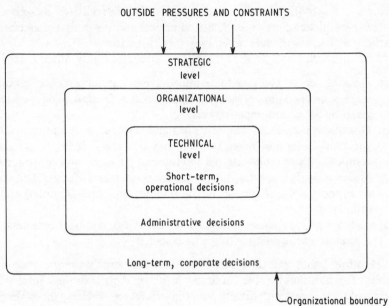

Fig. 3.1 Levels of organizational activity

(c) Organizational

This level of the organization is sandwiched between the other two. Managers and specialists at the organizational level mediate between strategic and technical managers and co-ordinate their work. They have to find compromises between the long-range issues which are the province of the parent organizations and the immediate operational problems of the task force. The organizational managers, partly in the shape of contracts managers, bridge the gap between the project team and the parent firms, looking for expedient solutions to problems for which there are often no 'right' answers.

These three levels of activity tend to merge and overlap, especially where the project is small. The same managers may perform parts of all three roles. In the case of large projects, the three levels are likely to be sufficiently distinct to be carried out by different individuals. Moreover, they may be executed relatively independently of one another, suggesting a break in the chain of command – another departure from the classical principles of organization. Petit contends that this break is a reality and this is most likely so when the task-force approach to production takes the team away from the parent firms. A project organization becomes a separate entity – isolated for much of the time from the influences of parent firms.

Indeed, it is possible to envisage the project as a microcosm of any one of the

68

parent firms, with its own strategic and organizational levels. There is doubtless some truth in this idea, but nevertheless a properly co-ordinated project should function primarily at the technical level. Unless the parent firms can influence project decisions, it is unlikely that the project will contribute to the long term objectives of the firms involved.

A recurrent problem when the project's short-term problems are allowed to dominate managers' time is that strategic issues are neglected. It is important that managers recognise the dangers of spending too much time solving operational difficulties.

A project structure is, then, primarily *technical* in purpose. It is concerned with bringing together a diversity of materials in a sequence of operations. The materials are at various stages of processing from 'raw' to 'ready-fabricated'. Some of the problems of combining them into a finished building were dealt with in Chapter 2. But successful integration also demands *human* skill and energy. These can be vital to the technical success of a project.

It was emphasized in Chapter 1 that the material and human inputs to the project are derived from a large number of different firms. Some of their contributions can be made in parallel with other operations, but others have to await the completion of earlier activities. What is lacking in the building project is the long-run stability found in the mass-production and processing industries. Each building project calls for a more or less unique mix of inputs within a fairly tight programme.

Because of this, the established methods of organizing production which have been derived mainly from experience in military and mass-production organizations do not always work so well for building. The classical, no-nonsense approach to organizational design, with its organization charts and job descriptions, can still work well when there is a well-defined task that needs to be executed by a well-disciplined group. But it does not encourage much personal initiative or allow much freedom of choice. Even the way a job is performed may be closely prescribed.

As Snowdon has argued, the purpose of an organization should be to *facilitate* the tasks of people and make it possible for their work to be co-ordinated [6]. As more people become involved, the need to co-ordinate their contributions becomes greater, but care is needed to ensure that the project structure encourages and *supports* people in their tasks and does not place unnecessary obligations on them.

3.5 Differentiation and integration of tasks

Whatever form the project structure takes, an element of hierarchy is necessary for co-ordinating different operations, since the tasks themselves will be highly differentiated. That is to say, different people will specialize in different things. It has long been a tenet of organization theory that specialization leads to efficiency, by making more rational use of resources. Probably, it is also necessary in order to cope with the complexity of current building practices.

But specialization also leads to fragmentation and in building this fragmentation is very marked. Not only is there specialization within firms, but each firm tends to specialize. Thus, the organization of a project team involves contributions from many firms, specializing in design, financial management, engineering, building construction, heating, plumbing, and so on.

Within the parent firms, specialization leads to isolation and can cause co-ordination problems. The R & D laboratory of the heating and ventilation contractor may be annexed in an old country house, whilst top managers may sit in a high-rise block in the capital; production may take place anywhere the firm is willing to work, perhaps in several provincial towns.

Within the project team, specialization can lead to communications breakdown and a lack of appreciation of other members' problems and goals. The greater the differentiation of tasks within the project group, the more potential *conflict* there will be. There is then an urgent need for a co-ordinating mechanism which can draw the parts together and weld them into a cohesive whole.

Co-ordination is the central task of the project manager, who will use power, skills, rules and contractual obligations, networks of communication, and face-to-face consultation to pull together an effective task-force.

The parent firm, whether general contractor or specialist, may have a comparatively tight pattern of specialized roles and relationships. Procedures may be closely prescribed and communication channels well established. Probably, there will be an organization chart, showing links between roles and perhaps between products or locations (Fig. 3.2). It can be useful as a kind of map of the firm. It can reflect the stability and well-tried practices of a permanent enterprise.

But it can have its drawbacks too. Charts and job descriptions can soon become out of date. People may feel bound by the chart and unable to use initiative. If events are changing rapidly, the organization may be too inflexible to cope.

The structure of most organizations in the construction industry is a variation of the so-called *line and staff* arrangement. 'Line' implies that managers receive information and orders from their bosses some of which they pass on to their subordinates. 'Staff' are the specialists – engineers, accountants, estimators and buyers – who provide a service or back-up to the line managers who get the work done.

Some managers have line and staff responsibilities. The planning engineer has a line relationship with his boss and a staff relationship with the site managers. Exactly how the line and staff relationships work depends on how

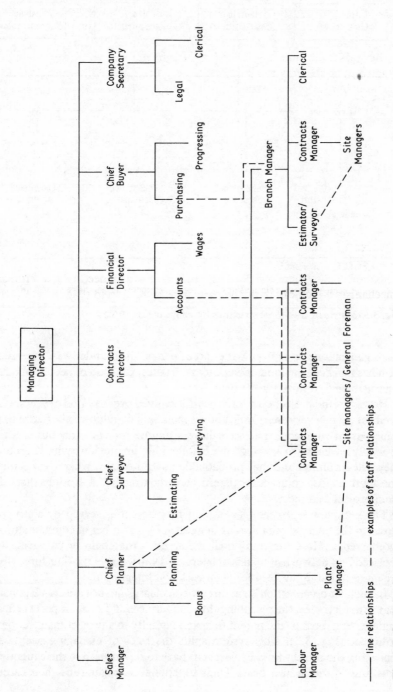

Fig. 3.2 Organization structure for large contractor

——— line relationships   - - - examples of staff relationships

Building Services Integration

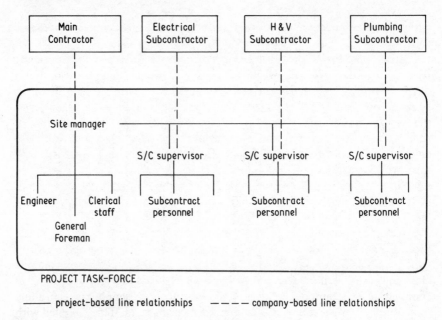

Fig. 3.3 Matrix or task-force structure for construction project

the organization has evolved – the sort of person the founder was, the size the firm has reached, the kind of work it undertakes, the kind of people who have been attracted to work for the firm.

However, the project task-force has not evolved over a period of years. It has been set up in a very short time and its members do not owe allegiance to the same parent company. The team have a unique task to carry out and they probably have not worked together before. They are not sure what difficulties they will encounter and they probably do not quite know what to expect from one another. They must come to terms with contractual obligations that differ from project to project.

This temporary project organization may be better served by a structure closer to the 'matrix' organization suggested by a number of commentators in recent years. Here the traditional hierarchy – the chain of command – is replaced by a network or matrix of lateral and vertical role relationships, which are more suited to the need for teamwork and integration.

In such an organization structure, the managers or supervisors responsible for the main trades, the plumbing, heating services and so on, report vertically to their 'line' boss in the parent firm and laterally to a project manager or co-ordinator (Fig. 3.3). This system splits the roles of managing people and managing the project task. Project staff have to report both to their functional boss and to the project boss. Their functional manager runs their careers,

72

whilst project managers 'bid' for their services, sometimes on a part-time basis [7].

Clearly, this approach can create problems of loyalty and commitment. Ideally, the individual's loyalty is to the parent company, but for the duration of the project, his commitment is to the task-force. This can be difficult to achieve, but a number of organizations in the construction industry have tried the approach, because they were dissatisfied with the traditional way of running projects. Some of the experiments with matrix organization have enjoyed a fair measure of success, although it relies on the willingness of those involved to break away from traditional practices and change their attitudes towards functional departments. The individual's primary allegiance has to shift from the discipline group to the task group, even though there are still many pressures from the parent firm to give priority to its needs.

Co-ordination is further complicated by the fact that the members of the project team vary over its lifespan. Unlike the factory-based organization, which can remain relatively static for long periods, the building project is changing continually, as it passes through the stages from inception to completion. The composition of skills and resources present in the team alters quite markedly over the space of a few weeks or months. This, coupled with the uniqueness of each project, means that new problems are always arising, calling for considerable time and effort by the task-force members and, especially, by the project manager.

3.6 The matrix organization and services integration

Monaghan [8] develops a model of the matrix organization specifically aimed at integrating building services. He argues that all project team members have direct line responsibility, instead of the traditional line/staff relationships. This ensures that they have total commitment to the task in hand.

Since the team members will have very different backgrounds and skills, it may be necessary to establish a few simple rules and procedures to ensure that members:

(a) Report direct to the project manager about all technical and organizational matters relating to the project
(b) Communicate with their functional heads in the parent companies on matters of staffing and administration which are not the responsibility of the project manager.

The matrix organization must be flexible. It should be structured in response to the type and complexity of the project. The management structure will depend on the *ratio* of services and specialist work to builder's work and the production levels that need to be maintained to meet the project completion date. The quality of available personnel must also be taken into account in deciding on the most suitable structure. Often the ability of an individual to work effectively in a team, to gain acceptance by others and to persuade them to accept his ideas, will be as important as his technical skill – and sometimes more important.

The traditional line-and-staff organization may not encourage the close co-operation and good communication that are essential to project success. Rigid job descriptions may be a disadvantage. Loosely defined, overlapping roles may encourage the kind of co-ordination that is needed. They can foster good, informal commmunication links to complement the formal communication system. The flow of ideas and information will be multi-directional and people will be better informed. They may become more supportive of one another.

Hunt [9] contends that informal, lateral communications are indeed *formalized* in the matrix structure because they are so important in bringing the task-force together as peers and focussing their attention on the problem.

The characteristics of a matrix organization for a building project are summarized in Table 3.1. It specifies the important variables in the design of such a system – its goals, timescale, task, people and environment. The variables will shift considerably from project to project, so that it is important to adopt a contingency or 'best-fit' approach.

Table 3.1 Project organization characteristics

PROJECT GOALS	Clear and short-term, compared with those of the parent firms. Specified as cost targets, time deadlines, quantities and standards of material, workmanship or performance. Most goals can be quantified and progress towards them measured.
TIMESCALE	Relatively short term. The lifespan of the organization is finite, with specific dates for commencement and completion of key stages and the project as a whole.
TASK	Variable in scope and technical complexity. Less repetitive than manufacturing tasks. Assembly of diverse range of raw and partly processed materials and components. High level of task differentiation, reinforced by custom and trade practice.
PEOPLE	Wide range of skills and backgrounds. Specialists, craftsmen, semi-skilled and unskilled. Willing to tolerate job mobility, low job security and poor working conditions.
ENVIRONMENT	Comparatively stable for the duration of the project, except for climatic environment which is highly variable, and labour market which fluctuates in response to local competition for manpower.

The resulting organization may be untidy but all that matters is that it works. Adherence to time-honoured rules of organization is of no value unless, at the end of the day, the project goals have been met.

References

(1) Handy, C. (1976) *Understanding organizations*, Penguin Books.
(2) Woodward, J. (1965) *Industrial Organization: theory and practice*, Oxford University Press.
(3) Burns, T. and Stalker, G. (1968) *The management of innovation*, Tavistock Publications.
(4) Lansley, P., Sadler, P. and Webb, T. (1975) Managing for success in the building industry. *Building Technology and Management*, 13 (7), 21–3.
(5) Petit, T. (1967) A behavioural theory of management. *J. Academy of Management*, 1, 341–50.
(6) Snowdon, M. (1977) *Management of engineering projects*, Butterworths.
(7) Thomason, G. (1973) *Improving the quality of organization*, Institute of Personnel Management.
(8) Monaghan, T. (1978) Services co-ordination. *Co-ordination of mechanical and engineering services*, Occasional Paper 16, Chartered Institute of Building.
(9) Hunt, J. (1979) *Managing people at work*, Pan Books.

4 · Management

4.1 Managers and their jobs

For decades, managers have tried to analyse their work in the hope of finding out how to do it better. Much of their attention has focussed on the similarities between their jobs. If managers do similar things, it should be possible to build up a picture of the 'ideal' manager for a construction project.

More recently, attempts to build stereotypes of the perfect manager have come under attack. Studies of managers and their jobs indicate that if we look at the differences between managers' jobs we find that management is really a family of jobs, in which individual managers may do very different things [1]. The site manager who has to co-ordinate the services work of five nominated firms with the operations of his own workforce may spend his time quite differently from the manager in charge of a textile mill, controlling a large direct labour force carrying out repetitive work.

The 'classical' view put forward by early management writers was that the manager *plans*, *organizes*, *co-ordinates* and *controls*. He decides what needs to be done and gets others to do it. He fits into a hierarchy of command that runs through the organization from top manager to worker. He often has five or six subordinates. He inspires loyalty and motivates people with rewards and punishments.

Many managers in the building industry cling to such classic descriptions of their work, but the reality does not always match them. More and more observers have noticed that managers do not always spend their time in the way the textbooks predict they will.

Mintzberg dismisses some of the myths of 'scientific management', claiming that little is systematic in the manager's daily work. Rather, his job is fragmented, varied and often interrupted [2]. Rather than being the thoughtful planner, the manager is primarily a trouble-shooter, negotiator and source of inspiration to others. His decisions are made quickly but they are not always good. His choices are often political and intuitive, his motives private and hard to define. It is true that managers plan and organize, make decisions and resolve crises, but most people cope with life in much the same problem-solving way, without thinking of themselves as managers.

Nor is it sufficient to look at the skills managers use as the distinctive feature of their jobs. Certainly managers rely heavily on skills for dealing with people, handling information, coping with breakdowns and deciding what to do next –

but so do many other people in their daily work.

What distinguishes managers from others is not primarily the tasks they perform or the skills they use, but the organizational *setting* in which they operate. Managers are given authority to run a unit towards some specified end. To achieve this, the organization gives them *power* over others in the system.

But running a business or department has become complex. Managers have to cope with many conflicting demands and constraints – some technical, others legal or human. Increasingly, the speed of change means that yesterday's solutions will not work for today's problems. The manager has to look for fresh answers and cope with novel problems.

Of course, everyone has problems to solve but the managerial problems tend to be less structured, harder to define and intractable. What constitutes a 'satisfactory' outcome to a managerial problem is often difficult to specify, especially in construction where the product is often 'one-off'.

4.2 The manager and production

The site manager's responsibilities differ from job to job, but broadly his concern centres around smooth, efficient production. Typically, he will be responsible for such tasks as:

(a) Site establishment and organization
(b) Production planning and engineering
(c) Resource control
(d) Review and measurement of progress, cost and quality
(e) Integration of builder's and building services work

The list can be expanded to include tasks for which the site manager has partial responsibility, such as purchasing, wages and incentives. The analysis is not exhaustive and, importantly, some tasks fall between the components identified above.

Some tasks are more far-reaching than others. They are of *strategic* importance, not to the parent firms (Chapter 3) but certainly to the project team. They are concerned with designing the operating system of the site. This includes the initial site establishment and organization, the location of major plant, materials storage and temporary accommodation. Production planning and parts of production engineering (such as setting out) also have a vital effect on overall performance and can therefore be included in this category.

The tasks which relate mainly to the day-to-day running of the site are at the *tactical* or operational level. The measurement of work executed, quality and cost – and decisions about material stock levels – are mostly (although not always) examples of tactical issues.

Whilst the strategic decisions are essential to the achievement of overall objectives, especially those of the parent organizations, the tactical decisions can have a marked effect on how efficiently these goals are achieved. A bad decision relating to one nominated subcontractor may affect the successful integration of all the building services work, with repercussions throughout the later stages of the project.

Moreover, the manager's tasks change markedly as the project moves through its lifespan. Unlike the largely repetitive operations supervised by the factory manager, each stage of a building project makes different demands on the manager. In the early stages, the manager will be involved in the direct supervision of the main building trades, with which he will usually have a high degree of familiarity. Later, his role shifts to that of co-ordinator of a number of specialist trades, many of which will be subcontracted and about which he will often have only limited knowledge.

These tasks can be managed more easily if production is planned systematically at the outset and progress monitored regularly. This involves setting targets, giving and receiving information, collaborating with other personnel, and using appropriate procedures and techniques. Planning and monitoring progress is so important in the integration of building services work that it merits greater attention and this is given in Chapter 5.

Yet, however thorough the planning, the manager is still faced with numerous problems. Brian Fine realistically points out that *uncertainty* is not a brief intrusion into a predictable sequence of operations. Rather, the opposite is true. For most building projects, periods of certainty are brief and rare intrusions in a sequence of unforeseen events and difficulties [3].

Organizing production in a factory is relatively straightforward, in that output levels are often determined by machine speeds or well-defined work practices. On the construction site, however, production is subject to variability from many causes. The main cause is the shift in the structure of tasks as the project moves through its life-cycle.

John Morris [4] identifies the main tasks of the manager on site as:

Keeping things going – ensuring a continuous flow of work

Coping with breakdowns and failures – when the continuous flow of work is interrupted.

If he is running things properly, the manager will try to anticipate breakdowns before they threaten continuity and skilfully avert them where possible. According to Morris, the experienced site manager will often be a master of procedures, rules (including rules-of-thumb) and regulations, gained from years of practical involvement.

Increasingly, running things properly depends on the manager having access to a considerable amount of *information*. Indeed, a large proportion of the manager's problems will either arise because of lack of information or will be difficult to resolve because of it. With building services work, the manager has a further problem with information. He may not only have difficulty in obtaining it, but he may find it hard to *interpret*.

Among other things, the manager will want to know how the services contractors intend to organize their work. He may find, however, that they have not committed themselves to paper. There is evidence that some managers prefer to keep their plans in their heads [5]. There is a strong case for committing to writing the key information relating to the organization of a project, so that tasks and resources, both of the Main Contractor and Services Subcontractors can be properly organized and systematically related to a timescale.

As mentioned in Chapter 2, computers are increasingly being used to assist managers with these aspects of his work. It is a subject that will be discussed in more detail in Chapter 7.

4.3 The manager and power

To be effective, the manager must be able to influence the behaviour of others. This presents special difficulties on the building site, where the manager has to exercise power over groups of workers, some of whom are employed and paid by – and thus owe their allegiance to – specialist contractors.

The manager must therefore examine carefully what sources of influence are available.

4.3.1 Resource power

The manager has control over resources or rewards that other people seek. He does not pay the wages of subcontract personnel, but he sanctions payments to the subcontractor and thereby has some indirect power over the people on site. Sometimes, but not always, he may have some influence over whether a subcontractor is employed again.

Resource power is seldom popular. People dislike the idea that their co-operation can be *bought*. However, if the manager can reward good performance by authorizing prompt settlement, this can contribute to *reinforcing* desired behaviour on the part of subcontract staff. There is, however, a subtle relationship between resource power and other forms of influence, so that control of resources may create little power, unless other forms of power are used in support.

4.3.2 Position power

This is sometimes called 'legitimate' power and stems from the manager's role or position in the project team. Others recognize that the manager has the right to give orders, control resources, inspect work and reject it if substandard. Position power must be underwritten by the influential members of the organization, otherwise such influence will be greatly diminished.

Position power, once established, gives the manager control over some important assets, notably *information*. The manager is the focal point in the communications network and can control the dispersal of information. Information displays synergy – the whole is often greater than the sum of the parts. In the information 'jigsaw', the parts are largely meaningless until they are put together.

The manager has access not only to information, but to individuals, groups and organizations, and the expertise, power and resources they possess. Above all, the manager has the acknowledged right to decide how the work is organized, to initiate communications and take action when things are not running smoothly. These are powerful influences over other people's behaviour.

However, subcontract personnel may be more impressed by the position power of their own supervisors and the Main Contractor's manager may have to look elsewhere for sources of power.

4.3.3 Personal power

Some managers are fortunate enough to have the personality, presence or charisma to influence others without recourse to extrinsic power bases. Such influence can stem from the manager's appearance, manner, poise, confidence or warmth – or more often, a combination of such factors.

Some managers rely on personal power to influence subcontractors, but such power can be ephemeral, elusive and temporary. It works sometimes and with some people. It should not be relied upon to replace position power but can usefully supplement it.

4.3.4 Expert power

Technical skill or knowledge gives the manager power over those who lack it. Most managers have some expertise in relation to their subordinates and use it to reinforce their position.

However, the manager often lacks such expertise in relation to specialist Subcontractors and can therefore be at a disadvantage. Indeed, the Subcontractor's site supervisor may be able to exercise expert power over the site manager, by virtue of his specialist skills and knowledge of building services.

The site manager must try to minimize this counteractive power if he is to retain control over the building services operations. He can do so partly by strengthening his other power bases and partly by becoming more knowledgeable about the subcontractor's work and the technology and skills it demands.

4.3.5 Physical power

This is power based on threat and the fear it induces. Few business organizations rely on such power, although many day-to-day transactions rely very temporarily on the threat of coercion as a very potent source of influence. The picket line can be viewed as an overt example of such power, often used as a last resort when other power sources have been exhausted. The manager will not normally regard physical power as part of his armoury of influence methods.

The manager should review his power from time to time. He should observe how others are affected by his power. They may accept it, ignore it or rebel. Broadly, people respond to power in three ways:

(a) Compliance

Some people comply with the manager because they perceive that it is worthwhile to do so. Force, reward, rules and procedures often result in compliance.

(b) Identification

Some people adopt the manager's proposals because they admire or identify with him. The charismatic manager may obtain co-operation in this way. It is an enjoyable phenomenon but the manager has to recognize that people may become too *dependent* on him.

(c) Internalization

The individual adopts the manager's proposals as his own. This form of commitment is most useful to the manager, for it is self-maintaining and fosters independence. But it is hardest to achieve, especially in building where new teams are constantly being created and relationships take time to establish.

The Subcontractor has split loyalties. To internalize the project goals, subcontract staff must set aside their commitment to the parent company and, perhaps, other customers who want their services (and may be prepared to pay more for them).

To elicit the co-operation of subcontract personnel, the manager must use a combination of contractual rules and procedures, rewards and sanctions, managerial skills and personal power. Which methods to use, and when, will largely depend on the task or problem concerned, the organizational setting or the people involved. Some of these issues are dealt with later in this chapter and in Chapters 5 and 6.

4.4 The skills of the manager

A lot has been written about managerial skills, but comparatively little is based on experience in the building industry. One study which did investigate the skills used by managers in building firms highlighted the importance which such managers attached to *social skills* [6]. These skills are central to leadership, motivation, communication and the co-ordination of people into effective teams.

The construction managers interviewed stressed the need to:

(a) Deal with people as individuals, taking account of personality and ability differences.
(b) Keep people informed, involve them in the task and foster a sense of co-operation and teamwork.
(c) Communicate clearly and show positive leadership.
(d) Show an interest in people and be willing to help them cope with work problems [7].

Such skills help establish good relationships with peers, subordinates and subcontract personnel. They result in a network of contacts which bring about action and the timely exchange of information and instructions. Thus, social skills are vital in achieving effective integration of building services within the building fabric.

The site manager should recognize that he has a special problem when exercising social skills with subcontract personnel. He cannot assume that they share the same values and attitudes as those of his own staff. Differences in the training of building services engineers and operatives, together with personality and skill differences which stem from alternative vocational choice and interests, can mean that the manager is dealing with different 'breeds'. The kind of behaviour which gets results when he applies it to his own subordinates may not elicit the same response from a building services supervisor. One cannot generalize, but there does seem to be some support for the argument that people in different jobs do behave differently and hold different attitudes. Moreover, people tend to adopt stereotyped behaviour, or at least move towards a stereotype of the competent practitioner, in their chosen field.

Other skills are important in managing a building project, but their potential cannot be realized fully if the manager fails, in human terms, to pull together a cohesive team. The integration of building services demands an understanding by all concerned of their mutual and individual problems and such awareness can only stem from good human relationships.

The skill most often ranked highly after social skill is that involved in *decision-making*. Most building industry managers seem to attach considerable importance to the ability to reach reasonably good, 'snap' decisions. Speed in decision-taking seems often to be more important than the quality of the decision reached. Partly this is because delayed decisions often mean idle resources, but some managers believe that quick decisions are expected of them. They are afraid of losing the respect of others (and hence control) if they hesitate in giving advice or issuing directives.

There may be some truth in this view, but it may also be partially a myth. Textbooks have always stressed, and often overemphasized, the importance of decision-making in managerial work. Managers may feel that they are judged primarily on their ability to make up their minds quickly and act. Sometimes this is necessary, but often a problem not properly thought out will be 'solved' by a poor decision which will bring no credit to the manager, however quickly it was reached.

With regard to building services work, the manager's decisions will often be organizational rather than technical. The technical problems will mainly be resolved by the services designers and the subcontractors involved. The manager will sometimes make organizational decisions unilaterally, but the value of involving specialist personnel should not be overlooked. In production groups and task force teams, group decisions are sometimes better than individual ones. There are several reasons for this, including:

(a) Groups can generate more information and ideas than one person and the ideas may be better. People can point out one another's mistakes.
(b) The range of experience and skills which a group brings to bear on a problem is greater.
(c) Making a group decision can have a strong motivating effect on the members and increase their commitment to the course of action decided.

On the other hand, group decision-making can be difficult and time-consuming. Envisage a site meeting between the Main Contractor's manager and four Subcontractors' supervisors. Many things can make the meeting ineffective, for instance:

(a) The group may be unable to reach a consensus. This could arise from conflicting personalities, differing goals or viewpoints, or lack of understanding of one another's problems.
(b) Failure to recognize and use the expertise and wide experience of the group. One member may dominate the discussion and stifle effective exchange of ideas.
(c) Too much time may be spent talking about issues which are tangential or irrelevant to the decision.

83

(d) The decision may only matter to one or two of those present. The others will 'switch off', resent their time being wasted or become counterproductive in the discussion.

Sometimes, the manager must make decisions on his own. Before doing so, however, he should consider what effect they will have on the Services Subcontractors.

Various writers have identified the stages involved in reaching a decision, but it must be said that, for many simple decisions, these stages are passed over very quickly and often without conscious thought. Broadly, making a decision involves:

(a) Clarifying the problem

Why is the decision needed and what are the goals to be achieved? What limitations or constraints affect the manager's freedom of decision?

(b) Analysing the alternatives

What information is needed and where can it be obtained? Is only one course of action feasible or are there viable alternatives?

(c) Choosing the optimum decision

Which course of action makes most sense in technical, financial or human terms? Who must be informed of this decision?

Here again, computers can be of assistance in providing the information immediately, as long as the manager follows the stages outlined above.

Most of the manager's decisions will be tactical ones. Individually, they will not necessarily affect overall objectives a great deal. But collectively, they can have a significant impact on project performance.

4.5 Leadership

Almost everyone agrees that skilful leadership is central to most managers' jobs. Certainly, the management of site operations will rely heavily on the leadership given, since the co-ordination of groups of people – both direct and sub-contract labour – is essential for achieving the goals of the project team.

It used to be thought that certain *personality traits* or personal characteristics, acquired largely through breeding or social background, were the basis of effective leadership; but the evidence has not given much support to this belief. Some investigators turned to *leadership style* and tried to discover which style worked best. Their results conflicted. Democratic or people-centred leadership became popular in the 1950s and 1960s but overall the evidence indicates that autocratic leadership is not always inferior to the more participative form and, indeed, works better in some situations.

The current view is that effective leadership depends on a number of conditions relating to the *leader*, the other people in the *group*, the *task* they are doing and the *setting* in which they operate. Leadership style is therefore specific to the situation. Someone who makes a good leader of a football team may not succeed in creating team spirit on a building site. We must look at a particular site and the people involved if we want to identify the right aproach for the leader.

The general Contractor's work is variable, each project posing fresh problems of resources and sequences of activities, so that programming is often difficult. The task demands considerable flexibility, yet the need for teamwork is high for successful integration of trades and specialisms. An autocratic leadership style may not be the most appropriate for many building projects.

A more democratic leader, who involves his team in problems and decisions, may get better results, although not necessarily all the time. Some team members may have little desire for participation and prefer to leave the decisions to the leader. Others may find such involvement essential for job satisfaction or motivation.

To select the right approach to leadership, the manager must analyse the situation asking the questions in Table 4.1.

In their study of twenty-five building industry firms, Lansley, Sadler and Webb also argued for a management style to suit the situation [8]. Specialist contractors tended to undertake work which was perceived as being more structured and predictable, suggesting bureaucratic control and a tighter leadership style. General Contractors, on the other hand, executed work of a more variable nature, calling for flexible, 'organic' management. A democratic leader might be more effective in such circumstances.

Leadership of groups within organizations is always going to be a vital ingredient, but the role is a highly complex one. At one stage, organization theory started to play down the importance of the leader in favour of group decision-making, control systems and structures. However, current trends are beginning once again to highlight the importance of the individual leader, but in the modified roles of catalyst, co-ordinator or spokesman.

There may be no 'ideal' leader, but there are certain requirements which seem important for leadership, namely:

(a) Skill at differentiating among people and situations, in order to respond to their specific needs
(b) Tolerance for ambiguous situations and ability to handle open-ended problems
(c) A clear self-concept, which will tend to go with confidence
(d) The setting of reasonably high standards, both for himself and his group
(e) Regular use of feedback to the group on their performance
(f) Plenty of energy, enthusiasm and motivation.

Building Services Integration

Table 4.1

What kind of leader am I?	Does my power come from position, personality, expertise or control of resources?
	Do I like making decisions on my own and do others accept them?
	Do I listen to others and take their advice?
	Do I delegate to others and give them enough responsibility?
What kind of people are working for me?	Do they want to participate in solving problems and making decisions?
	Do they want responsibility and autonomy?
	Can I *rely* on them to get on with the job without close supervision?
	What expertise do they have?
What sort of task?	Does it need to be tightly programmed?
	What are the priorities for effective control of the task?
	Is it straightforward and repetitive or will unpredictable problems keep cropping up?
The setting.	How powerful am I? Does the firm give me the authority and support I need?
	Do the group members like me?
	What kind of influence do I have over building services personnel?
	Are we a cohesive team? Compact? Are there conflicting goals?

Such attributes are particularly important in integrating building services work, where the manager lacks some of the power bases discussed earlier.

4.6 Motivation

There have been many attempts to explain what motivates people. Some argue that motivation occurs within a person, whilst others believe that one person can motivate another. Many attractive and simple explanations of motivation

86

have been put forward, but they have proved very difficult to back up with sound evidence.

Some managers have long believed that people can be motivated by *rewards*, yet financial incentives have often failed to secure consistent improvements in effort. Others have assumed that *job satisfaction* will increase motivation, but it is not that simple.

Another approach has been that motivation is triggered by a range of human *needs*. People are attracted to work on a building project because it gives them an opportunity to satisfy some of their wants. But co-operation is necessary if the combined needs of those involved are to be met. Many factors inhibit such co-operation, so that the focus shifts to conflict. Conflicts arise in organizations because the various groups fail to get what they want in return for their efforts. Conflict cannot be eliminated and indeed may sometimes be productive, leading to improved practices; but it is important that the manager tries to keep it within acceptable limits.

Conflict can effectively reduce motivation, so that the management of conflict is one of the key tasks of 'running things properly'. Conflict between the Main Contractor and Subcontractors can arise from differing goals and priorities, disagreements about tactical decisions and arguments about contractual obligations. At the root of such problems is the simple fact that the *needs* of the parties involved either differ or cannot be achieved by the same means.

Conflict can also stem from inequalities in the way groups are treated and these become apparent in the status and reward differences between the main trades and building services specialisms on site.

A complication is that individuals have different needs and these change over time. The manager can rarely find one solution to the problem of motivating everyone on site; they all want different things.

Broadly, the manager can approach motivation in two ways. One is to look at the motivating forces outside, or *extrinsic* to, the individual's task. This aspect of motivation has been misused because many managers have not clearly understood the conditions under which reward systems operate.

The second kind of motivation is that which is internal, or *intrinsic*, to the task a person is performing. Whilst this approach to motivation has been much discussed, some commentators have taken a rather superficial view, failing to deal with these factors in a comprehensive way [9].

Our understanding of these two aspects of motivation rests on the work of two separate groups of psychologists; though it is useful, for purposes of analysis, to deal with extrinsic and intrinsic factors separately, in practice the two are inextricably linked.

Ideas about extrinsic motivation owe much to Skinner's work on behaviour [10]. He found that performance of a task is more likely to be repeated when a reward is given. Rewards need not be financial or even tangible and can consist of anything valued by the individual – a word of praise, a nod of approval, or a hint of future promotion. In our everyday lives in the building industry, we are continually rewarding or failing to reward others, often without being aware of it.

Why have bonus schemes often failed to motivate? There are many issues at stake here but what Skinner found about the repetition of rewards is not widely known among managers. He noted that if the performing/rewarding cycle is repeated regularly – at a set time or after a fixed quantity of output – there is a gradual decline in the level of activity. Rewards given unpredictably result in continued motivation to repeat the task. This is how gamblers are rewarded; they do not know when they are going to win ... and they do not always win.

Also, when a person's behaviour is ignored, there is a tendency for it not to be repeated. Thus, the absence of suitable rewards can lead to reduced effort, unless intrinsic motives can take their place.

If one wants to increase motivation by offering rewards external to the task, the reward has to be something valued by the individual doing the work [11]. While some people prefer tangible things like cash, others are happy with a promise of future gain, although what the individual considers rewarding varies over time.

Reward systems often have unpleasant connotations, implying some controlling person offering or withholding returns to less influential persons, but it is important to remember that it is a two-way process. Workers and subcontract employees reward the manager by being friendly or co-operative, or simply by turning up for work. Alternatively, they can withhold such 'rewards' and may lower the manager's motivation!

The site manager has a special problem with building services personnel. He simply may not have control of the kinds of reward they want. Certainly, he will not directly control their wages and conditions of employment, and his impact on their prospects for future employment and promotion are usually minimal.

Yet people will often work at a job even when rewards are poor for no other reason than the pleasure of doing it. What makes such a job intrinsically motivating? Bruner identifies three factors: natural curiosity about the task, a drive to become more competent and a social need to co-operate with others towards a common objective [12].

Curiosity is aroused when a task is unclear, unfinished or uncertain. Attention is usually maintained until that problem has been resolved. A craftsman or engineer may be motivated in this way when he has an unusual production detail to work out. However, for the worker's attention to be sustained, tasks must become a little more demanding or at least different from previous tasks. If the task is too easy, the worker will become bored; if it is too difficult, he will become frustrated. Setting the right task for each worker is clearly difficult and demands ingenuity and imagination on the part of supervisors and managers.

The building industry has an advantage over mass production and processing industries in that its work centres around a wide diversity of projects which contain considerable novelty and scope for flexibility. But the manager's scope may be limited by rigid job specifications or demarcations imposed by unions. If managers could structure work more flexibly, the pay-off could be considerable, both in terms of motivation and of job satisfaction. The manager would have to set targets which would stretch each operative a little either in the nature of the task or its degree of difficulty. Building services supervisors could do this too but there is little scope for the site manager to motivate subcontractors' personnel by this means.

'We get interested in what we get good at' is how Bruner explains the second element of intrinsic motivation, the drive to become more competent. Unless a person develops some degree of competence, it is difficult to maintain interest in the task. To achieve this, the individual must have some measure of how well he is doing and this relies on being given clear *targets* and *feedback* on performance. A vague target which extends far into the future offers little scope for motivation. Again, the site manager has limited influence over subcontractors' personnel, except in terms of overall targets and these have only limited value in stimulating motivation.

It is, however, known that people have 'competence models' – individuals with whom they work, whom they respect and whose standards they would like to make their own. These models need not necessarily be in positions of authority and there is scope here for the manager to influence building services staff.

People can be extremely loyal to their 'competence models' and may use them to sound out their ideas. The site manager should be aware of such influence processes and use them where possible.

The third component of intrinsic motivation is the need to respond to others and work towards a common goal. The project can provide a common objective and different people will make different contributions. Some will be natural leaders and where possible should be given the chance to exercise their skills. Others can contribute useful ideas – or simply do what is asked of them. It is in cultivating these interlocking roles, both among direct labour and subcontract personnel, that the manager can foster the sense of working together as a team. If people can see *how* they contribute to the group's effectiveness, they are likely to become more highly motivated.

Construction work is carried out almost entirely by small squads of operatives in trade or specialist groupings. Within such teams, co-operation tends to arise naturally. However, co-operation *between* such groups is often less evident and provides scope for considerable improvement under good management. Co-operation with, and among, subcontract 'gangs' will be fostered where the manager is able to demonstrate that collaboration benefits *everyone* involved and not just the Main Contractor. The manager can do this by emphasizing that the project goals represent a strategy, within which the varying needs of the contributors, individuals and organizations alike, can be *reasonably* well satisfied, providing they work together.

There is no simple answer to how to motivate people. The manager will find that they have different needs and their needs change over time. Money may be the most important reward for some workers but for many others, their efforts will be triggered in other ways. The manager cannot hope to motivate everyone all the time. But, by fostering a team spirit, offering challenging and interesting tasks and giving as much freedom within jobs as possible, he may gain better results than by relying solely on bonus schemes and the authority of his position.

4.7 Communication

The success of a project team depends not only on the calibre of its members but on the quality of the links between them. It is the process of communication that links the participants together and helps to weld them into a working community.

Poor communication has long been regarded as a serious problem in construction. The fragmentation of the industry has been blamed for some of the structural communication failures, but there are other problems. Individuals, including many managers, are lacking in communication skills, so that messages are misunderstood or ignored.

An adequate communication structure or network is essential for effective control. In construction, this network must operate within the project team and between the team and its parent organizations. Communications must provide for:

(a) Instructions and information to flow between the project team and the parent organizations, using formal channels of comunication as specified in the relevant forms of contract. Informal communications will supplement these links, but must not be used where they might give rise to contractual problems (see Chapter 6).
(b) Instructions and information to flow within the project task-force from the co-ordinating levels to the workface with provision for feedback at each level.
(c) Information about task requirements, problems and resources to flow from work-teams to the co-ordinating level and, where appropriate, laterally among the Contractor's trades and building services teams.
(d) The structure of communication to change as the demands of the project shift over its lifespan.

Clearly, if a communication system is to work well, information and instructions must be accurate and well-communicated. To achieve this, the manager needs a reliable information system and skilful communication. Yet many managers are less efficient in their communication than they realize [13]. Some of the common failures stem from:

(a) Overloading

The manager gives or receives too much information at once, causing incomplete comprehension or confusion.

(b) Choice of method

Managers do not always stop to think how to communicate most effectively. Sometimes an oral message is best, but at other times a written or pictorial message is more suitable.

(c) Distance

The physical separation of groups in the building process means that less communication occurs. Moreover, much of it is not face-to-face and valuable non-verbal cues are missing.

(d) Distortion

Parts of the message may be ignored or misinterpreted, either because the receiver does not want to see or hear them or because the sender leaves out items or contaminates the message. Sometimes this is deliberate where, for instance, there is lack of trust or the sender feels that his power position is threatened.

(e) Immediacy

The more immediate communications blot out the less immediate. For instance, a telephone call disrupts the manager's conversation with a services subcontractor; this in turn causes a letter to be put aside and, perhaps, forgotten.

(f) Status

People of lower status or authority may find it difficult to communicate with those in higher positions. The opposite can also be true but probably less often.

(g) Emotion

The emotional overtones of a message can distort or overshadow the factual content.

(h) Lack of clarity

What is obvious to the sender may not be at all obvious to the receiver. The use of jargon, woolly language and ambiguous words can lead to communication failure. This is a common source of communication breakdown between the

Main Contractor and specialist Subcontractors. The technical language of some of the specialist trades may be largely incomprehensible to many of the Main Contractor's staff. Moreover, even plain words like 'design', 'tolerances' and 'equipment' may conjure up very specific images in the minds of different members of the project team.

To be a skilful communicator, the manager must recognise that each communication takes place in a more or less unique situation. He must respond to that situation and be sensitive to how it differs from previous situations. He needs all his social skills to respond in this way, for the receiver must *understand* what is being communicated, *accept* it and often be *persuaded* to act upon it.

What the manager can do to improve communications with Services Subcontractors is to:

4.7.1 Encourage two-way communication

Listen to what the Subcontractor's supervisor has to say and try to understand his viewpoint and problems. Give opportunities for seeking clarification of information and instructions. This may take time, but it will be well worthwhile.

4.7.2 Keep the communication as direct as possible

The more people between the manager and the person who ultimately has to act on the message, the greater the chance of misunderstanding. However, the manager must consider whether such action could give rise to contractual problems and must use judgement.

He should have a thorough knowledge of the impact on formal communication of the Subcontract Forms and Consultants' Forms of Agreement applicable to the project.

4.7.3 Use more than one communication channel

Most formal communications occur through the hierarchical links and links with expert/specialist groups within the project team. The manager should use informal links based on friendship and peer groups to prepare the ground for, or underline, the formal communication.

4.7.4 Take advantage of modern technology

The advent of microcomputers and their ability to provide information immediately and simply, both on site and in the office, can alleviate many of the communication problems identified above. However, care must be taken not to overestimate their usefulness. If the communication system is wrong and the information inaccurate, then computers can actually make communications worse.

Clear communication is inseparable from willing co-operation. Managers who attach most importance to their technical role often underrate this link [14]. Such managers are frequently slow to realize when people misunderstand them and fail to recognize that people may be suspicious of their motives. Sensitivity to a situation, coupled with appropriate attitudes, can be just as important as verbal skill.

References

(1) Stewart, R. (1976) *Managers and their jobs*, Pan Books.
(2) Mintzberg, H. (1976) The Manager's job: folklore and fact. *Building Technology and Management*, **14** (1), 6–13.
(3) Fine, B. (1979) Production management. *Management in the construction industry* (ed. R. Burgess), Macmillan.
(4) Morris, J. (1979) Developing managers for the construction industry. *Management in the construction industry* (ed. R. Burgess), Macmillan.
(5) Mintzberg, H., op. cit.
(6) Fryer, B. (1977) *Development of managers in the construction industry*, MSc. thesis, University of Salford.
(7) Fryer, B. (1979) Managing on site. *Building*, **236** (25), 71–2.
(8) Lansley, P., Sadler, P. and Webb, T. (1975) Managing for success in the building industry. *Building Technology and Management*, **13** (7), 21–3.
(9) Fryer, B. and Fryer, M. (1980) People at work in the building industry. *Building Technology and Management*, **18** (9), 7–9.
(10) Skinner, B. (1953) *Science and human behaviour*, Collier–Macmillan.
(11) Higgins, M. and Archer, N. (1968) Interaction effects of extrinsic rewards and socio-economic strata. *Personnel and Guidance J.*, **47**, 318–23.
(12) Bruner, J. (1966) *Towards a theory of instruction*, Harvard University Press.
(13) Handy, C. (1976) *Understanding organisations*, Penguin Books.
(14) Stewart, R. (1979) *The reality of management*, Pan Books, pp. 92–7.

5 · Production planning

As was seen in the previous chapter, the planning of production is an extremely important aspect of project management deserving detailed discussion. In this chapter we shall firstly consider the overall philosophy of planning and then show how this is put into practice. Finally, we shall concentrate on those aspects of planning specifically related to services integration.

5.1 The need for planning

On the majority of building projects, the part of contract planning that receives least attention is the period during which the majority of services work takes place. Planners are very confident when it comes to preparing detailed sequence studies of the work involved in making the building weathertight. However, the remainder of work, either because of inadequate information or lack of knowledge of what is involved, is planned with less confidence and in less detail. Normally the work is arbitrarily split into 'first fix' and 'second fix' operations which are tentatively linked to the 'internal finishings' and then everything is left to providence. This applies to both Main and Subcontractors who, if they do carry out any formal planning, do not always ensure that their plans are compatible.

Chapter 2 has already described the close interrelationship of the building elements and the services installation. Similarly, several studies have shown that the integration of work carried out by Services Subcontractors is a task that gives site management most concern. Furthermore, building services installations contribute a relatively high proportion of the total project costs nowadays. Consequently, more energy should be devoted to the planning of the internal work than to the earlier stages of the contract.

'Why bother planning, when a programme is out of date from day one?' is the retort that is too often heard. Unfortunately, it is an attitude that is hard to alter since it is based on some popular misconceptions about planning.

What is planning? Who should plan? How should we plan? The remainder of this chapter will attempt to alter these misconceptions by answering these questions and showing how important planning is in the integration of services work.

94

5.2 Basic planning concepts

5.2.1 The planning–control cycle

Planning can be considered as a series of decisions based on objectives and information which result in the conscious determination of a course of action. Without planning, any activity will be random and the result will be chaos.

However, if planning is to be made effective there is another important ingredient – that is *control*. Control is the process of continually comparing the plan with reality thus enabling management to periodically review the situation and, if necessary, modify the initial plan in order to achieve the overall objectives.

Planning and control are thus two inextricably linked processes that follow the cyclic pattern shown in Fig. 5.1. Moreover, the frequency of the cycle will depend on the level of management concerned as shown in Table 5.1.

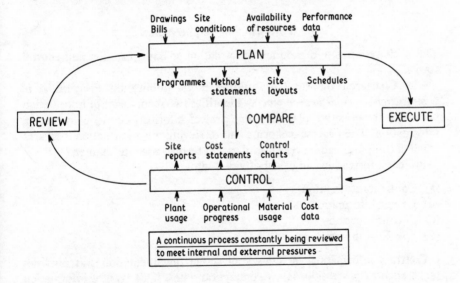

Fig. 5.1 Planning–control cycle

Table 5.1

Level of manager	Frequency of cycle
Contracts Manager	Monthly
Site Manager	Weekly
Foreman/Ganger	Daily

95

5.2.2 Objectives

In order that the cycle operates effectively there must be objectives, sometimes called targets or standards. The terminology is relatively unimportant. What is important is that some means is provided for comparing the plan with reality and this must be measurable.

The objectives themselves form a hierarchy of interrelated long-term and short-term objectives depending on the time span or frequency of the planning–control cycle. For instance, the main contract will provide senior management with an overall objective for the project, usually this will be the completion date and the total budgetted cost. This can then be broken down into monthly targets to enable monthly control to be carried out. The monthly sections of the plan will then in turn provide the basis for more detailed plans with weekly targets to enable the site manager to carry out his weekly control and similarly for the foreman or ganger to control on a daily basis.

5.2.3 Information requirements

The cycle requires and produces information at both planning and control stages.

The Chartered Institute of Building in its publication *Programmes in Construction – a guide to good practice* identifies two main forms of information necessary for effective planning, i.e. project information and construction information. The process of storing and retrieving this information is an area where a computer can be very useful as will be discussed in Chapter 7.

Project information can be sub-divided into:

(a) Contract information
(b) Design information
(c) Site information
(d) Specialist information.

Contract information includes contractual documentation and provides items such as possession dates, completion dates. This type of information rarely changes during the course of construction.

Design information consists of the various working drawings, specifications, and other schedules and reports issued by the various members of the design team. The degree of completeness of this type of information has a considerable bearing on the accuracy and effectiveness of any construction programme.

Site information is peculiar to each site and can affect working methods quite considerably. It is the responsibility of the Main Contractor to obtain such information.

Specialist information emanates from the various specialists involved, e.g.

Nominated Subcontractors and should include lead times, attendances, working methods and sequences, and any dependency on calendar dates.

Construction information can be further sub-divided into production information, reference information and factual information.

Production information includes the targets, durations and working methods used by the contractor to plan and schedule his operations. Such information is normally contained in some form of library and is specific to each contractor.

Reference information is obtained from periodicals and learned papers providing the contractor with information regarding innovations, changes in legislation, etc.

Factual information includes such items as weather records, crane capacities and other facts that are useful in determining working methods.

All this information is combined to produce a contract programme and other associated documents, such as method statements and site layouts. These documents are then used as a basis for subsequent control purposes.

To control the plan, information, obtained from site allocation sheets and measurement of completed work is compared with the information produced at the planning stage to indicate any discrepancies between the plan and reality. Not only should this comparison indicate immediate discrepancies but also any trends in the discrepancies, i.e. will things get better or worse?

It must be obvious that the information used at both the planning and control stages of the cycle must use the same basis to enable comparison to take place. It may not be quite so obvious but it is equally important that information should also be quick and easy to prepare. If this is not so, two things will happen. Firstly, the costs of operating the system will be greater than any potential savings; and secondly the information will be too historic to enable management to take action.

Another problem with information is that it is not always available when required in the detail that is required. This applies particularly to design information and consequently dictates the accuracy with which the planning can take place.

5.2.4 Decision-making

Decision-making has already been discussed in detail (Section 4.4) as an important managerial skill and is very relevant to the planning–control cycle.

The plan is the product of decisions which require interpreting data of differing degrees of 'completeness' and accuracy (as stated in Section 5.2.3), and the subsequent evaluation of alternative methods and resource requirements to achieve the objectives of the plan. Similarly, the control and review stages of the cycle require the interpretation of information and the evaluation of future courses of action. In other words 'what happens if?' The

97

eventual success of the plan is, therefore, highly dependent on the skill of the people making these decisions.

To summarize: *A plan is only as good as the reliability of information used, the degree of control exercised and the quality of thought applied.*

5.3 The people involved

It should be evident from the previous section that planning is just as much an attitude of mind as the use of any particular method or technique. Moreover, it is an attitude of mind that should permeate throughout the entire organization – whether it is the Main Contractor, the Nominated Subcontractor or the project organization itself. Without the co-operation of everybody involved in the project any attempts at planning will be frustrated.

Many Main Contractors now employ planners to produce method statements, site layouts and programmes with the result that planning has become a specialist function. These planners often plan the work in isolation at head office, send the information to the site team to help control the work and then subsequently visit the site at irregular, infrequent intervals. The result is an alienation between those who plan and those who control the work. This poses communication problems which, in turn, makes the planning–control cycle less effective.

It is important that both the planners and the site staff get involved at stages of the contract thus altering the role of the planner from that of a functional specialist, to that of an educated scribe who records the ideas and decisions made by the construction team in such a way as to make the cycle effective.

Specialist Subcontractors, with a few exceptions, carry out less formal planning that the Main Contractors and yet the manner in which they execute their work can pose considerable constraints on the remainder of the work. Similarly, unless they are aware of the constraints imposed on them by the Main Contractor, they may make planning decisions, formally or informally, totally unsuited to the needs of the project as a whole. It is difficult to say which is more important, the constraints imposed by the Main Contractors or those by the Subcontractor. Normally it will be determined by the needs of the situation and will always be some form of compromise. The important thing is that this potential conflict is recognized from the outset and dealt with by negotiation throughout the contract.

5.4 Procedures and techniques

Having discussed the philosophy of planning, it is now time to see how this can be put into practice. We shall do this by considering it in terms of procedures and techniques.

5.4.1 Procedures

The procedures involved in planning can be considered at various stages in the time span of the project.

(a) Pre-tender planning

Pre-tender planning is primarily aimed at providing accurate information for estimating purposes; whilst it may seem desirable to complete this planning before the estimate, it is usually necessary and expedient to carry out the two tasks in parallel. Whilst the ultimate expression of the pre-tender plan will normally take the form of a programme with supporting documentation, this is preceded by some careful investigative work which results in a pre-tender report. Thought should be given to the engineering services work and the firms nominated to do it, although at this stage it may be minimal, particularly if the Nominated Subcontractors are not known, as is sometimes the case.

Apart from its value in estimating, the information contained in the pre-tender report can form the basis of more detailed contract planning, should the tender be successful. An example of the format of this report is illustrated in the Code of Estimating Practice published by the Chartered Institute of Building. Whilst the emphasis of the report will vary from project to project, the content will tend to centre around the details of:

   (i) Ground conditions and topography
  (ii) Disposal of spoil, and local facilities
 (iii) Site access, transport and temporary roads
 (iv) Layout of the site
  (v) Security and storage of own and Subcontractors' resources
 (vi) Accommodation and temporary services
 (vii) Availability of resources
(viii) Method appreciation for main work items
 (ix) Information relating to designers and consultants
  (x) Information relating to local and statutory authorities
 (xi) Information about engineering services work.

(b) Pre-contract planning

When the contract has been awarded, the successful Contractor must carry out several important tasks in a very short space of time. Clients often expect a speedy commencement of site operations and the Contractor may be under pressure to make a start before the work has been planned and organized. The preparation of a detailed check-list helps to ensure that no important task is overlooked. The effort expended by the Contractor during the short time from the award of the contract to the commencement of work on site can have a considerable impact on the subsequent running of the project and its success in both financial and human terms. The importance of giving the site manager

Building Services Integration

adequate information and establishing a team spirit among those who will be committed to the project has been emphasized in Chapters 3 and 4. All too often, the opportunity of involving the Services Subcontractors and ensuring their commitment to the project, is not fully utilized and integration problems are thereby neglected, until they become critical.

Key activities will include:
(i) Appointment of contract personnel
(ii) Establishment of head office support
(iii) Preliminary meetings of project team members
(iv) Contract analysis
 – temporary services and accommodation
 – working methods
 – relationship with subcontract work
 – key dates
(v) Preparation of contract programme
(vi) Setting up procedures for communication and feedback.

(c) Detailed planning

On commencement of work on site the site manager will have to carry out the following tasks:

(i) Identify the sequence of operations to be undertaken
(ii) Check production information and setting out
(iii) Ensure availability of resources
(iv) Provide advice, information and instructions
(v) Review progress, cost and quality of the work.

This is normally referred to as detailed planning and helps keep contract planning alive and responsive to change. If the project is very straightforward the site manager can make short-term plans mentally, but as the size and complexity of the project increases, the amount of information to be handled and the interaction of the effects of decisions taken can escalate; it then becomes essential to plan on paper. The timespan of a detailed plan will vary from one week to four or five weeks. The latter may be called a monthly plan or a stage plan, although the stage plan can sometimes refer to a plan for a specific set of operations (such as first-floor slab) and may then be longer or shorter than the monthly plan, depending on the operation. In general, detailed planning tends to centre around trade operations. Services Subcontractors tend to do their own detailed planning.

Weekly plans provide the site manger and his foremen with the most direct and detailed means for organizing and reviewing the day-to-day operations on site and with the last chance to call forward outstanding requirements if delays are to be avoided. Few site managers, however experienced, will be able to remember all the relevant information which will enable them to efficiently organize every task in the week ahead.

A weekly plan can help control the work by indicating:

(i) Information requirements – any outstanding information requirements for the next week's work will now be urgently required. The manager must take immediate action if delays are to be avoided.
(ii) Work sequences and methods – the relationships between the tasks to be performed and the methods agreed for executing them need to be finalized. The sequence and methods for working, including materials handling, should be communicated to the operatives involved, through their respective foremen.
(iii) Workforce – the number and skills of operatives needed to perform the week's work must be decided. Each week, the size and composition of the labour force will need to be reviewed, not only to take account of the tasks programmed for that week, but to include outstanding work resulting from earlier setbacks.
(iv) Resources – materials, mechanical plant and consumables not already on site may need to be progressed. Some delivery arrangements may need to be finalized or changed.

These three stages of planning are interrelated (see Fig. 5.2) and, as discussed in Section 5.2.1, require the commitment of everybody in the project management team.

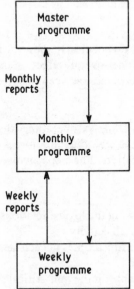

Fig. 5.2 Interrelationship of general, monthly and weekly plans

101

Building Services Integration

5.4.2 Techniques

The techniques most appropriate to the integration of services work are:

(a) Bar charts
(b) Activity on the arrow diagrams (network, analysis)
(c) Activity on the node (precedence diagrams).

(a) Bar Charts

The bar chart is the most widely used technique in the building industry, primarily because it is quick, and easy to prepare and understand. This facility is very useful in short-term planning, i.e. the monthly, weekly and daily plans described in Section 5.2. It also communicates the concepts of sequence, timing and resource allocation very clearly; it is therefore often used to produce the eventual work schedule when other techniques have been used.

A typical bar chart (Fig. 5.3) displays the start, finish and duration of each activity to a time scale together with a facility for recording the actual progress. This is normally done by dividing the bar horizontally and recording planned progress in the top half and actual progress in the bottom half.

More comprehensive bar charts show the following:

(i) Labour requirements (both operationally and weekly)
(ii) Plant requirements (both operationally and weekly)
(iii) Material delivery dates for each operation
(iv) Dates when drawings and information must be available to carry out each operation
(v) Holiday periods.

Unfortunately, bar charts do not clearly show the interrelationship between the activities and hence the net overall effect of any delays. Neither does it indicate any trends in discrepancies between planned and actual progress.

(b) Network analysis

This is more applicable to complex operations than the bar chart and the greater rigour, imposed by the logic diagram, forces the planner to think more about interrelationships involved. The steps involved in producing a network are:

(i) List the activities
(ii) Produce a network showing the logical relationship between activities
(iii) Assess the duration of each activity
(iv) Determine the start and finish times of each activity
(v) Identify the *critical path*
(vi) Calculate the *float* available on the non-critical activities.

102

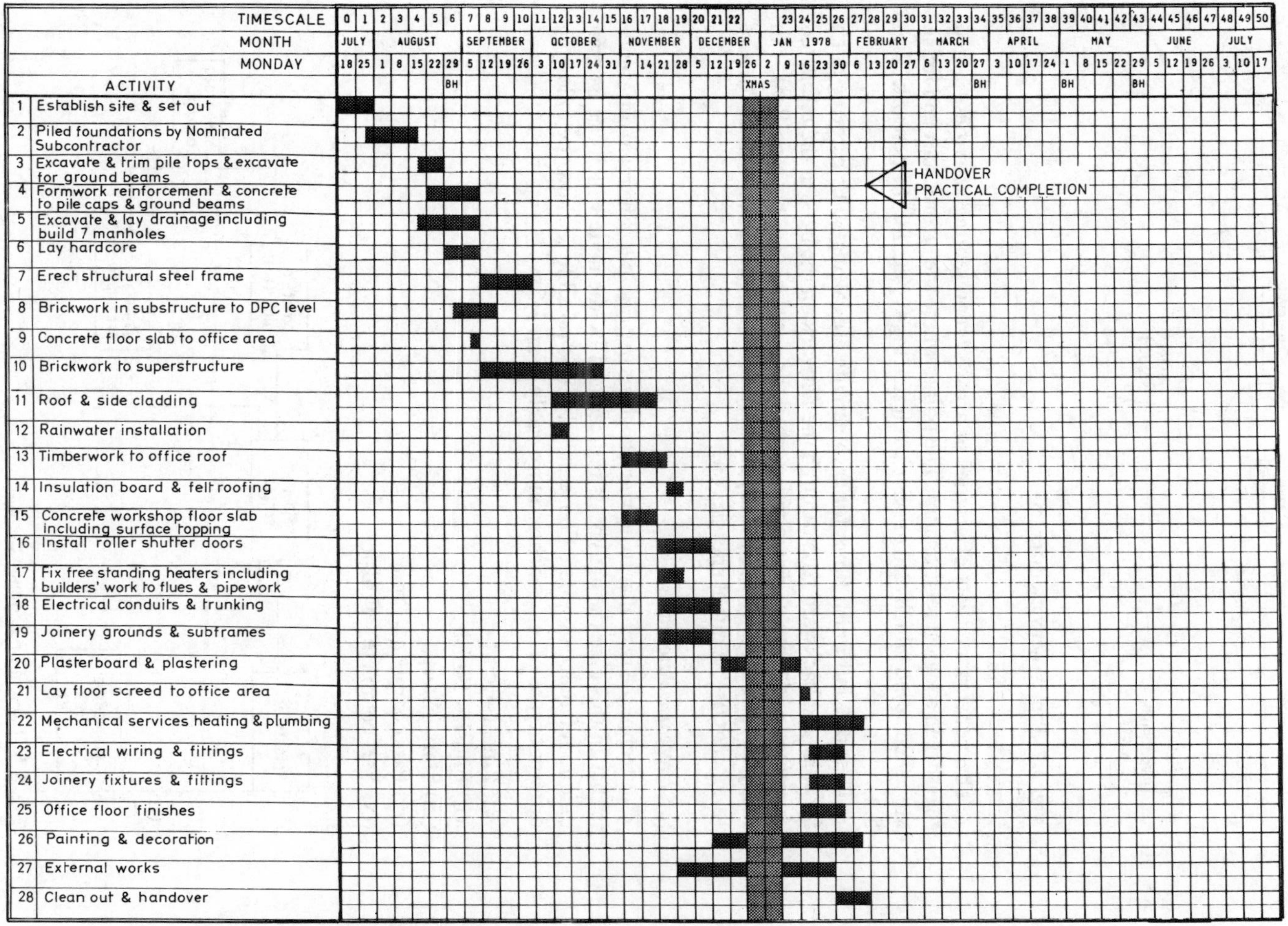

	TIMESCALE	0	1	2	3	4	5	6	7	8	9	10	11	12	13	14	15	16	17	18	19	20	21	22	23	24	25	26	27	28	29	30	31	32	33	34	35	36	37	38	39	40	41	42	43	44	45	46	47	48	49	50
	MONTH	JULY	AUGUST				SEPTEMBER				OCTOBER					NOVEMBER				DECEMBER				JAN 1978				FEBRUARY				MARCH				APRIL				MAY				JUNE				JULY		
	MONDAY	18 25	1 8 15 22 29				5 12 19 26				3 10 17 24 31					7 14 21 28				5 12 19 26				2 9 16 23 30				6 13 20 27				6 13 20 27				3 10 17 24				1 8 15 22 29				5 12 19 26				3 10 17		

ACTIVITY

1. Establish site & set out
2. Piled foundations by Nominated Subcontractor
3. Excavate & trim pile tops & excavate for ground beams
4. Formwork reinforcement & concrete to pile caps & ground beams
5. Excavate & lay drainage including build 7 manholes
6. Lay hardcore
7. Erect structural steel frame
8. Brickwork in substructure to DPC level
9. Concrete floor slab to office area
10. Brickwork to superstructure
11. Roof & side cladding
12. Rainwater installation
13. Timberwork to office roof
14. Insulation board & felt roofing
15. Concrete workshop floor slab including surface topping
16. Install roller shutter doors
17. Fix free standing heaters including builders' work to flues & pipework
18. Electrical conduits & trunking
19. Joinery grounds & subframes
20. Plasterboard & plastering
21. Lay floor screed to office area
22. Mechanical services heating & plumbing
23. Electrical wiring & fittings
24. Joinery fixtures & fittings
25. Office floor finishes
26. Painting & decoration
27. External works
28. Clean out & handover

HANDOVER / PRACTICAL COMPLETION

XMAS

Fig. 5.3 Typical bar chart (from *Programmes in construction – a guide to good practice*, CIOB)

Building Services Integration

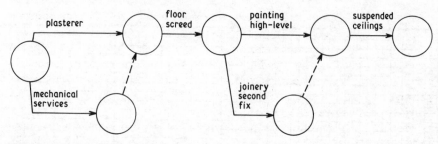

Fig. 5.4 Typical network diagram

The network consists of a series of arrows, representing activities, joined together in a logical relationship. The points where the arrows start and finish are called *events* which also provide a referencing system for the network (Fig. 5.4).

The start and finish times for each activity are calculated by carrying out a forward and backward pass through the network on the basis of the estimated durations and from this, activities which are critical, i.e. have no float, can easily be identified. Consequently, management can easily see which activities to concentrate its initial energies on.

(c) Precedence diagrams

This technique is similar to network analysis in principle. The main difference is that in this case the activity is represented by the node which has its own unique reference number. Consequently, it is possible to show the following different types of relationships more easily (Fig. 5.5):

(i) Finish – Start
(ii) Finish – Finish
(iii) Start – Start
(iv) Part complete – Start
(v) Part complete – Finish

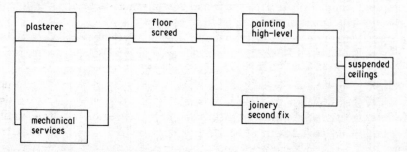

Fig. 5.5 Typical precedence diagram

104

As with network analysis it shows interrelationships and critical activities clearly and is a very useful management tool.

However, both are not without their disadvantages. Firstly, as suggested previously, they do not readily illustrate the concept of time. Secondly, activities on site do not always have a well-defined start and finish and cannot always be represented accurately by a network, although this is less true with precedence diagrams.

Because all the techniques discussed have their disadvantages the most appropriate answer is to combine the advantages of networks and bar charts. This can be done initially by using networks to get the logic right and then bar charts to communicate the ideas to the respective management personnel.

Such an approach provides the basis of the majority of standard computer packages now available in this field (see Section 7.4.1).

5.5 Planning for integration

The discussions so far have concentrated on general planning philosophy and practice, and it is fair to say that if all the recommendations were carried out services integration would be made easier. However, it is possible to be even more specific and identify the particular aspects of planning relevant to services integration.

The first prerequisite is a well-prepared programme based on a network or precedence diagram (Fig. 5.6). This should identify all the activities relevant to the Services Subcontractors' work. Not only does this assist the Services Subcontractor plan his work accordingly but it also provides a means for subsequent control of the services work by the Main Contractor.

The Main Contractor should explain his overall approach to the services Subcontractor, stressing the interrelationship of the building services work and the remainder of the project, whilst appreciating the fact that the Services Subcontractor wants to keep his site visits to a minimum. Either party may have to change some of its initial thinking because of lack of knowledge of the other's requirements. In fact the final solution will inevitably be some form of compromise and the ease with which that compromise is achieved will depend upon the willingness of both parties to co-operate.

Special attention needs to be given to linking locations such as corridors, staircases, lobbies etc. Designers tend to cram them full of equipment, whilst everyone uses them as thoroughfares. The Services Subcontractor working in such areas can become frustrated at the continual interruptions which, if not moderated, can have an adverse effect on progress. Similarly, it is also necessary to discuss confined areas such as toilets, ducts, etc., which allow only one trade to operate at a time. Both sides will need to be clear on times when the site is open, on weekend working, and on the need to work longer hours to achieve specific objectives, such as those stated by the Client. These might

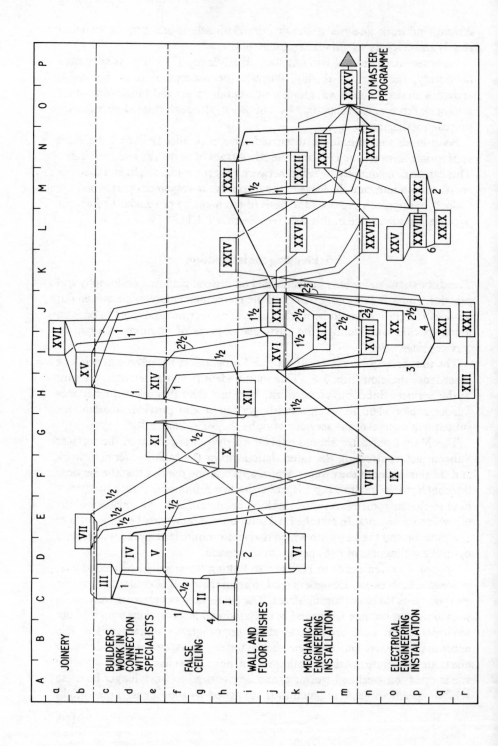

Key to boxes in Fig. 5.6

(I) Steelwork upper grid
(II) Plasterboard and tape to plenum chamber ceiling
(III) Lower birdcage scaffold
(IV) Adjust scaffold for electrical seal floor, lay polythene
(V) Chase out for electrician and wall conduit
(VI) Drop pipework for fire extinguisher
(VII) Fix timber battens and wall lining
(VIII) Fix integral light fittings and wire along high level trays
(IX) Electrician lay main and sub cables on concrete floor
(X) Set out and fix suspended environmental ceiling grid
(XI) Dismantle middle area birdcage scaffold
(XII) Paint walls and floors to seal computer room
(XIII) Electrician lay special trays and cables S & T room floor void
(XIV) Blockwork and brickwork to dwarf walls
(XV) Internal wall linings and dismountable partitions
(XVI) Steel cover floor supports
(XVII) Joiner fix doors ironmongery internal glazing and keycard system
(XVIII) Fix conduit and wiring for heat detectors in floor void
(XIX) Fix pipework to fire extinguisher system in floor void
(XX) Fix conduit wiring and fire alarm detectors in floor void
(XXI) Electrician fix P.D.U. boxes and test
(XXII) Electrician final fix S & T room floor void
(XXIII) Access floors with anti-static and floor level extract grilles
(XXIV) Fix suspended ceiling to plant control room and decorate
(XXV) Fix high and low level cable and wire and connect to others including substation and telecommunications
(XXVI) Fix heat detectors and grilles in computer floor
(XXVII) Electrician fix switches alarms, etc., to walls and remove temporary lighting
(XXVIII) Electric wiring to controls and motors
(XXIX) Auto scan
(XXX) Commission control panel
(XXXI) Fix and seal environmental celing plenum chamber
(XXXII) Fix air conditioning grilles, fire sensors and outlets
(XXXIII) Initial test air conditioning environmental system
(XXXIV) Fix lighting diffusers, etc.
(XXXV) Occupational balancing prior to computer equipment

Fig. 5.6 *(Opposite)* Precedence diagram showing interrelationship of Service Sub-contractors work and the remainder of the work (from *Programmes in Construction – a guide to good practice*, CIOB)

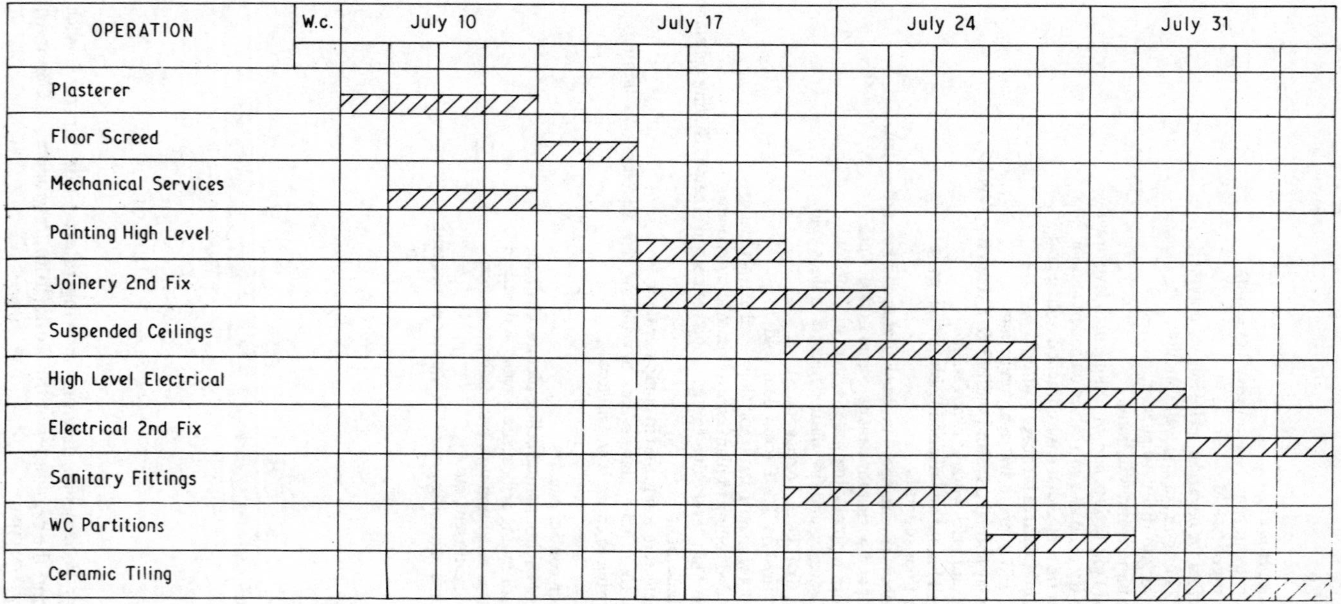

OPERATION	W.c.	July 10			July 17			July 24			July 31		
Plasterer		▨											
Floor Screed			▨										
Mechanical Services		▨											
Painting High Level					▨								
Joinery 2nd Fix					▨		▨						
Suspended Ceilings							▨	▨					
High Level Electrical										▨			
Electrical 2nd Fix											▨		
Sanitary Fittings							▨	▨					
WC Partitions									▨	▨			
Ceramic Tiling												▨	

Fig. 5.7 Short-term bar chart used for integrating Services Subcontractors work

relate to services links to existing premises and implications on availability.

Finally, the programme must be checked against known periods of notice required by any of the parties; delivery periods and the implications of testing and commissioning.

Short-term bar charts (Fig. 5.7) based on this programme can then be used for initial and subsequent regular meetings of the production teams of both Main Contractor and Services Subcontractor to discuss, and review progress of, the services work and any associated problems. It is recommended that these meetings are held separately from, and preferably before, the regular site meetings with the Architect at which more general items and progress are discussed.

Apart from being good practice it is advisable to follow these recommendations in order to ensure that the relevant contractual requirements are met as will be seen in the next chapter.

Further reading

Harris, F. and McCaffer, R. (1977) *Modern Construction Management*, Granada Publishing.
Oxley, R. and Poskitt, J. (1980) *Management Techniques Applied to the Construction Industry*, Granada Publishing.

6 · *Contractual constraints*

6.1 Standard forms of contract

The Architect, Services Consultant, Main Contractor and Services Subcontractor enter into a contract, either with the Employer or with one another. These contracts are normally based on a standard form that has been formulated by the respective professional institutions and trade organizations. The contractual relationships created by these standard forms (Fig. 6.1) should form the basis of any project organization structure as discussed in Chapter 3.

Some of the terms and conditions of these standard forms require interpretation and often rely on previous court judgements. Consequently, it is another aspect of management that requires specialist knowledge. However, it is essential that all members of the project organization acquire a working knowledge of the standard forms in order that they can perform their managerial roles and responsibilities effectively, and recognize situations when they should obtain specialist help.

It is the aim of this chapter to provide this basic knowledge as it applies to the integration of building services. Consequently, it concentrates on the JCT Standard Forms of Contract for Nominated Subcontractors. It also refers to JCT Standard Form of Main Contract, the RIBA Conditions of Engagement

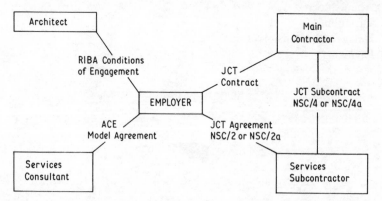

Fig. 6.1 The standard forms of contract affecting the organizations involved in services integration

110

Table 6.1 The JCT Standard Nominated Subcontract Forms

Tender NSC/1	Standard Form of Nominated Subcontract Tender and Agreement
Agreement NSC/2	Standard Form of Employer/Nominated Subcontractor Agreement
Agreement NSC/2a	Agreement NSC/2 adapted for use where Tender NSC/1 has *not* been used
Nomination NSC/3	Standard Form for Nomination of a Subcontractor where Tender NSC/1 has been used
Subcontract NSC/4	Standard Form of Subcontract for Subcontractors who have tendered on NSC/1, executed agreement NSC/2 and have been nominated by NSC/3
Subcontract NSC/4a	Subcontract NSC/4 adapted for use where NSC/1, NSC/2 and NSC/3 have *not* been used.

for Architects, and the ACE Conditions of Engagement as appropriate. It is not proposed to discuss the terms and conditions of these documents clause-by-clause as this is done quite adequately elsewhere, [1, 2]. Instead, the contractual obligations of the various parties will be discussed in relation to the following topics:

6.2 The process of nomination
6.3 Information flow
6.4 Damage and loss to services installation and equipment
6.5 Attendances
6.6 Variations
6.7 Delays and extension of time
6.8 Payment

6.2 The process of nomination

A Nominated Subcontractor is defined as an organization whose final selection and approval for the supply and fixing of any materials or goods or the execution of any work is reserved to the Architect. This is done by means of a prime cost sum in the Bill of Quantities.

The various forms are summarized in Table 6.1. In the majority of circumstances the Architect or Consultant Engineer invites tenders from the Services Subcontractors using the standard form of tender NSC/1 and this in turn involves the Employer and the Services Subcontractor entering into a standard form of agreement NSC/2. The successful Subcontractor is nominated using NSC/3 and enters into a contract with the Main Contractor (subcontract NSC/4).

In some instances contract documents can state specifically that the above method is not to be used in which case the Architect nominates a Services Subcontractor who enters a standard form of subcontract NSC/4a which includes an appendix containing the various matters contained in tender NSC/1.

6.3 Information flow

The co-ordination of design information has already been identified in Chapter 1 as a common problem and this is mainly due to the contractual responsibilities of the Architect and the Consultant engineer. The RIBA Conditions of Engagement specifically state that the Architect should integrate any work carried out by the Consultant Engineer. However, the ACE Conditions of Engagement does not confirm these responsibilities. Consequently, the Consultant engineer may be less enthusiastic about teamwork and integration.

The model forms can also lead to problems involving the provision of builders work drawings. According to the ACE Conditions of Engagement, they are not the responsibility of the Services Consultant and the task is normally left to the Services Subcontractor.

After the contract has commenced, a set of plans produced by the Architect, upon which are superimposed the location of services equipment and the routes of service pipes, conduits, etc., are usually provided for the Main Contractor and Services Subcontractor to co-ordinate their respective work.

6.4 Damage and loss to the services installation and equipment

Equipment and materials for services installations are easy to damage and, because of their relatively high unit cost, are ideal targets for pilfering. It is important therefore, that all parties are aware of their responsibilities in relation to these aspects.

The Main Contractor is responsible for any loss or damage to the Services Subcontractors' goods or materials if it is caused by fire, explosion or overflowing of water-tanks before they are fixed, whether or not the loss or damage is due to the negligence of the Services Subcontractor. He is also responsible for the services installation after it is fixed under all circumstances.

The Services Subcontractor is also responsible for any loss or damage to goods or materials before they are fixed if it is caused by any other cause than those itemized above.

6.5 Attendances

These are facilities that the Main Contractor provides for the Nominated Services Subcontractor and are referred to in the contract documents (NSC/4 Clause 27) as general and other attendances.

6.5.1 General attendance

This is provided free-of-charge by the Main Contractor and is deemed to include only the use of the Main Contractors' temporary:

(a) Roads
(b) Paths and pavings
(c) Standing scaffold
(d) Standing power-operated hoisting plant
(e) Temporary lighting and water supplies.

It also provides for the

(f) Clearing away of rubbish
(g) Space for the Nominated Subcontractor's own offices and storage of plant and materials
(h) The use of mess-rooms, sanitary accommodation, and welfare facilities.

The Nominated Subcontractor is, however, required from time to time, during execution of the Subcontract works, to clear away, to a place provided on the site, all rubbish from his execution of the Subcontract works and shall keep access to these works clear at all times.

6.5.2 Special attendance

These are specific items, (over and above the general items mentioned above) provided by the Main Contractor on the basis of details provided in NSC/1.
Such items could include:

(a) Carrying out any necessary unloading. This very often applies to large items of equipment which are part of the services installations and may be required to be delivered whilst the Services Subcontractor is not on site.
(b) Providing hoisting facilities. In some instances engineering services equipment can often include some of the heaviest items that require hoisting, in excess of the Main Contractor's requirements.
(c) Positioning items of equipment. As with unloading, this can often apply to items of engineering services equipment that may need to be built into the structure before the majority of the services work is executed;
(d) Special scaffold. If there is no appropriate scaffold to meet the Services

113

Subcontractor's requirements on site then he must give the Main Contractor details of his requirements.

Attendances are often a bone of contention at site level and it is imperative that all site staff of both Main Contractor and the Services Subcontractor are fully aware of their rights and obligations in this respect.

6.6 Variations

Variations are common to most projects and it is therefore important that all members of the project organization are aware of how they should be treated.

In the case of engineering services, most variations will emanate from the Services Consultant although variations relating to other aspects of the work may affect the Services Subcontractor's operations. It is important that they follow the channels already illustrated in Fig. 6.2.

Variations may also result in a claim for extension of time (see Section 6.7) and also be valued for extra costs as illustrated in Fig. 6.3. Both these possibilities require clear documentation and it is important that site staff are aware of the importance of collecting the appropriate information to substantiate such claims.

6.7 Delays and extension of time

Delays often occur on building projects for a variety of reasons and can affect the work of both the Main Contractor and the Services Subcontractor. If the delay affects the Services Subcontractor he should inform the Main Contractor, in writing, who should then inform the Architect. The Architect can then allow the Main Contractor to allow the Services Subcontractor an extension of time if the delay has been caused by:

(a) Variations
(b) Act or ommission by the Main Contractor or any other Subcontractor
(c) Delay of drawings
(d) *Force majeure*
(e) Exceptionally adverse weather conditions
(f) Strikes
(g) Inability to obtain labour or materials for unforeseen reasons.

Items (a), (b), (c) can also provide the basis for extra costs.

The preparation of these claims is a specialist activity but they do rely on information from site level. Consequently, it is important that the relevant site records are maintained accurately.

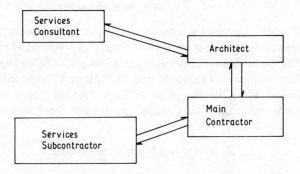

Fig. 6.2 Formal communication channels on building projects

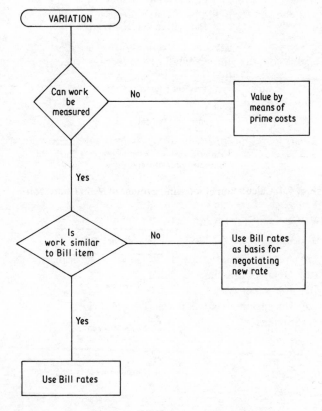

Fig. 6.3 Rules for valuing variations

Building Services Integration

6.8 Payment

The Main Contractor is usually paid monthly by the Employer within fourteen days of the receipt of an interim certificate prepared by his Quantity Surveyor. The certificate will normally include work done by the Nominated Services Subcontractor (Fig. 6.4) and the Main Contractor should pay him in accordance with Fig. 6.5. If there are any problems regarding dilatory payments by the Main Contractor to the Services Subcontractor then provision

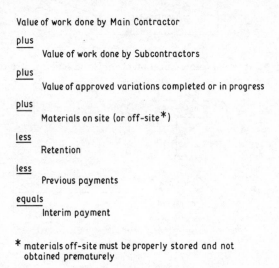

Fig. 6.4 Calculation of interim payment to Main Contractor

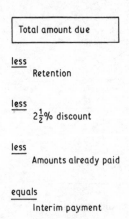

Fig. 6.5 Calculation of interim payment to Services Subcontractor

116

can be made for the Services Subcontractor to be paid directly by the Employer.

If the Services Subcontractor completes his work before the project is completed he can receive final payment. However, if any defects in the services installation are found between final payment to the Services Subcontractor and the issue of the final certificate for the entire works, then the Employer can ask the Services Subcontractor to remedy them.

Apart from these basic rules, most contracts allow for the fluctuation clause to apply, which allows for price increases. Consequently, the above calculations are modified by the application of agreed formulae.

Payment is another area of specialist activity which relies on accurate information from site, namely the measurement of work done and the quantity of unfixed materials.

6.9 Other areas of specialist knowledge

The terms and conditions of the standard forms of contract also include items such as insurances, determination of contract and arbitration. These items are very much specialist areas and are dealt with in detail elsewhere [1,2]. Consequently, if situations arise in these areas, management should seek specialist advice.

6.10 Managerial tasks and procedures

From the foregoing discussions it can be seen that some aspects of the standard forms of contract should be common knowledge to all members of the project organization, other aspects are specialist tasks relying on information from management and others are solely specialist in nature. This is summarized in Table 6.2.

Management must, therefore, carry out the following tasks and procedures in order to comply with its contractual obligations effectively:

6.10.1 Ensure correct information flow

All formal communications should follow the channels shown in Fig. 6.2.

6.10.2 Maintain appropriate records

In order to provide information for formulating claims, the following records should be kept and updated regularly:

(a) Drawings registers
(b) Receipt of Architect's instructions and variation orders

Table 6.2 Types of knowledge appropriate to general management and specialists in the JCT contract

Common knowledge for all management	(1) Formal channels of communication, (2) General and special attendances, (3) Responsibilities for storage and security of services equipment, materials and installation.
Specialist tasks requiring information from management	(1) Valuation of variations (2) Claims for extensions of time and/or extra costs (3) Payment of Interim Certificates and Final Accounts
Specialist knowledge	(1) Insurance (2) Fluctuations (3) Determination of Contract (4) Arbitration

(c) Materials stored on site for services installations
(d) Measurement of work done by Services Subcontractors
(e) Weather conditions
(f) Services Subcontractors site labour force
(g) Extra work and programme-changes as a result of variations.

Items (a) and (b) can be recorded on simple pro-formas with details of reference number, title, date received, as and when the drawings or variation orders are received. This requires diligence and accuracy as they may provide the basis of claims for both extra time and costs. It is also advisable to indicate sections of work and the relevant Services Subcontractors to which the drawings or variations apply. This will help information retrieval if any subsequent claims arise.

Items (c) and (d), are recorded on a monthly basis to assist in preparing interim certificates and require a systematic tour of the site with a check list of materials and items of work.

Items (e) and (f) can be recorded in a site diary.

Item (g) is the most difficult since it requires judgement on behalf of the site staff. The effect of delays on programmes are never easy to ascertain as the original programme itself normally consists of a set of interrelated operations. Consequently, a delay of, for instance, one week on a particular operation, does not necessarily mean that the entire project will be delayed by one week. The use of networking techniques described in Chapter 5 is very useful for such purposes.

6.10.3 Awareness of contract conditions

Management should be aware of the facilities that the Main Contractor is

118

required to provide for the Services Subcontractor. They should also be aware of their responsibilities regarding the storage, security and protection of equipment, materials and completed services work.

Finally, it should be said that contractual conditions only lay down minimum requirements. Consequently, the previous recommendations should only form the basis of any organizational or managerial tasks and procedures discussed in previous chapters. Similarly, it is always better to organize and manage the work without recourse to enforcing contractual rights and obligations. In this way good working relationships can be fostered, and hence co-operation and integration made easier.

References

(1)   Jones, G.P., *A New Approach to the (JCT) 1980 Standard Form of Nominated Subcontract*, Construction Press.
(2)   Duncan-Wallace, I.N., *Hudsons Building and Engineering Contracts*, Sweet & Maxwell.

7 · *Successful integration*

7.1 Roles and relationships

In Chapter 1 it was stated that the organization and management of a building project requires the co-ordination of a large number of highly-differentiated operating units whose roles and interrelationships may change over a relatively short period of time. It is this organizational setting that provides the framework for successful integration since the Main Contractor and the Services Subcontractor are two such operating units. Their differences can be summarized with regard to the following factors:

(a) The nature of the work they carry out
(b) The amount of time that they spend on the project
(c) The way in which they are organized
(d) The backgrounds, attitudes and experiences of their workforces.

These differences have to be recognized, and an appropriate set of roles and relationships created in order to accomodate them. This can be done by designing a formal organization structure in the following way:

(a) Determine the objectives of the project, both in overal terms and specifically in relation to the requirements of the building services installation.
(b) Create a project task-force to achieve these objectives using a matrix organization structure. This is a dynamic organization in which project team members report directly to the project manager on all matters relating to the project and communicate with superiors in their own organizations on other issues not relevant to the project.
(c) Produce flexible job descriptions in which roles overlap thus encouraging integration.

This should help overcome the problems of conflicting loyalties of the members of the Main Contractor and Services Subcontractors' staff and result in a communication network which will keep all members of the project better informed.

7.2 Techniques and procedures

A high proportion of technical, organizational and managerial problems can be

120

predicted before the work commences or have been experienced on previous contracts. In response to this, many well-established techniques and procedures have been devised to cope with them.

7.2.1 Techniques

An important requirement for successful integration is an effective production-planning system. Because of the complex interrelationship between the services work and the remainder of the work, such a system should be based on network planning, either activity on the arrow or precedence diagram. This is a technique which demands that the interrelationship of the services and building work be given serious consideration during the planning stages of a contract; it subsequently provides management with accurate information regarding the effect of any delays or changes that affect either the building work or the services work. It will be even more useful if both the Main Contractor and the Services Subcontractor use network planning techniques to plan their respective work thus making it easier to identify the interrelationship between their work.

The very nature of building work, however, results in many situations that are difficult to programme in any detail. These can be coped with by a careful use of meetings, both formal and informal. This facilitates two-way communication and allows group decision-making, both of which are useful in resolving integration problems. Such meetings should complement the formal site meetings attended by all members of the project task-force and should concentrate solely on matters relating to services integration. Consequently, they only require the attendance of the Main Contractor and the Services Subcontractors. The frequency of these meetings will, inevitably, vary depending on quantity and complexity of the services work at the time.

7.2.2 Procedures

The procedures necessary for successful integration can be divided into:

(a) Production-planning procedures
(b) Information flow procedures
(c) Legal procedures.

(a) Production-planning procedures

As stated in Section 7.2.1, a production-planning system based on network analysis is necessary for successful integration. However, this technique needs to be incorporated into an appropriate set of procedures if the system is to be completely effective. These procedures consist of:

(i) The formulation of a pre-tender report used in conjunction with an outline

121

programme. These can then form a base for initial negotiations with the Services Subcontractor if the Main Contractor is successful with his tender.

(ii) The preparation of a master programme, based on the pre-tender programme, before work commences on site. This programe should clearly show the interrelationship between the services work and the remainder of the work. Other pieces of information, e.g. key dates for the building becoming weathertight and the provision of 'heat-on', should also be indicated to act as 'milestones' for subsequent monitoring purposes.

(iii) An initial meeting between the Main Contractor and the Services Subcontractor to establish formal communications, attendances and other operational requirements.

(iv) The formulation of short-term programmes by both the Main Contractor and the Services Subcontractor, abstracted from the master programme. These short-term programmes can then be used as a control document for reviewing progress and act as a focal point for discussions at meetings (see Section 7.2.1).

(b) Information flow procedures

The flow of information between the Architect, Main Contractor, Services Consultant, and Services Subcontractor is another key factor in successful integration. In order to comply with contractual obligations, the formal channels of communication for information should be as described in Chapter 6 (Fig. 6.2). However, these formal channels need to be supplemented by informal communications in order to make the system dynamic. The most common type of informal communication in relation to services integration is between the Services Consultant and the Services Subcontractor. This is very useful if technical problems arise since both parties talk the same langauge. However, careful monitoring of such decisions is necessary in case there are implications for the rest of the work. Apart from the flow of technical information, there are other matters that affect services integration. Conflicting information on architectural and services drawings are common to most projects. Similarly, builders work-drawings to assist in the accurate location of holes are also a common cause of site problems. The use of transparent overlays in conjunction with a master drawing or layout drawings can be very effective in minimizing these co-ordination problems. The Building Services Research and Information Association also produce various publications [1, 2], which are extremely useful in determining space allowances for services elements and co-ordinating design information.

In addition to the technical information, there are other types of information to be communicated, e.g. information about task requirements, problems and resources. Such information relates to production and should be directed through the formal channels since the Architect and the Main Contractor are the major parties involved in any decisions on these matters.

(c) Legal procedures

The major legal constraint on the integration of building services is the JCT Contract and its associated Subcontracts. The formal communication channels necessary to comply with these contracts have been outlined above. However, there are other procedures that need to be carried out in order to ensure that contractual obligations are met. These procedures should include:

(i) Records of receipt of drawings, variation orders and Architect's instructions
(ii) Records of weather conditions
(iii) Records of the Services Subcontractors' site labour force
(iv) Accurate measurements of work done by the Services Subcontractors
(v) Accurate accounting of materials stored on site required by the Services Subcontractor
(vi) A systematic procedure for recording the effect of variations and delays relating to the services work.

Services integration is also affected by the Building Regulations. The main requirements relate to:

(i) Fire-stopping around pipes that pass through walls and floors
(ii) The prevention of fire-spread through suspended ceiling voids
(iii) The proximity of different types of services in ducts.

It is important that these requirements are known to members of both design and construction teams, and the use of a check-list itemizing these requirements would be useful in ensuring that they are considered.

7.3 Managerial style

As stated in Chapter 3: 'successful integration demands human skill and energy. These can be vital to the technical success of the project'. In fact a close analysis of Chapters 3 and 4 reveals an underlying theme of flexibility in the organization and management of building projects. The matrix organization takes account of informal relations between the Main Contractor, Services Subcontractor, Architect and Services Consultant. However, a manager's social skills need to be used in conjunction with this framework.

These human and social skills, or managerial style, include the art of leadership, the ability to motivate and the appropriate use of power. Their use is vital if the co-operation of the Architect, Main Contractor, Services Consultant and Services Subcontractor is to be obtained. Without this co-operation, integration is virtually impossible.

123

Building Services Integration

Unfortunately, achieving co-operation is hampered by the differences between the operating units already outlined in Section 7.1. Moreover, the Main Contractor has little control over many factors affecting the motivation of the Services Subcontractor's operatives. Similarly, the site manager has very little chance to exert any power over the Services Subcontractors apart from personal power.

These obstacles can be overcome by obtaining the commitment of the Architect, Services Consultant, Main Contractor and Services Subcontractor to the project goals and by emphasizing that these goals can satisfy everybody's needs. A democratic leadership style, in which services specialists are involved in all decisions relating to services integration, will also assist in obtaining their co-operation. Other means, such as sanctioning prompt payment to the Services Subcontractor, understanding the needs of the workforces of both operating units, becoming more knowledgeable about the Services Subcontractor's work and the technology and skills it demands, all contribute towards successful integration. Unfortunately, these recommendations are not easy to achieve and are often neglected with the result that integration is poor.

7.4 The use of computers

A recent report by the Building Services Research and Information Association [3] said 'It is considered that the use of computers will hold the key in the future to overcoming co-ordination problems, and that over the next decade we should utilize the power of the computer to rationalize and improve co-ordination procedures'. This is very true although computers should not be viewed as the panacea to all integration problems. There is a saying about computers: 'If you put rubbish in, you will get rubbish out'; it is well worth remembering.

Computers can perform calculations very quickly, they can store data very efficiently and in such a way that it can be manipulated to provide different people with information to meet their particular needs. They can also generate reports based on these calculations and data. More recently, the emergence of the silicon chip has added to this potential. The new generation of microcomputers possess the following advantages:

(a) Cheapness
(b) Portability
(c) Capable of operating in a normal working environment
(d) Easier to use
(e) Capable of providing 'on the spot' information
(f) Capable of receiving and producing data in a graphical form.

They are not, however, capable of making decisions, negotiating, leading or motivating. Consequently, it is important that problems are thought out properly first, and computers only applied in situations which can take advantage of their strengths, e.g. the techniques and procedures described in Section 7.2. The aspects of managerial style described in Section 7.4 can only be carried out by human beings.

7.4.1 Present-day applications

There are at present three areas in which computers can assist integration. They are:

(a) Network analysis packages
(b) Word processing
(c) Informational retrieval packages.

(a) Network analysis packages

It is now possible to have a microcomputer situated on site which can operate independently from any external sources. As a result, several software packages have been written, based on network analysis which enable site management to plan and control the work more effectively. Apart from a few minor variations, these packages operate in the same manner. Firstly, a network diagram is prepared, and durations and resources allocated to each operation. This data is then entered into the computer. The computer then performs all the necessary calculations to identify the critical path. Management can then request various reports including:

(i) Project bar chart indicating all the critical activities and the total float on non-critical activities
(ii) Short-term bar chart similar to the project bar chart
(iii) Resource histograms
(iv) Cash flow curves.

The most useful report to assist in services integration, however, is the selective report. This enables management to obtain a report, similar to the short-term bar chart but restricted to a specific trade or section of work. Thus it is possible for management to obtain bar charts for all the Services Subcontractors work and use it as a basis for monitoring their progress.

Because the computer can perform the necessary calculations very quickly and then generate any combination of reports automatically, updating the programme is very easy. The manager has simply to enter any changes of duration, sequence or resource, and leave the rest to the computer. The entire process takes approximately an hour compared with the few days it would take, if done manually. In this way it is possible to determine the effect of any variations or delays. Experience to date has shown that these reports have provided a focal point for all formal communications between the Main Contractor and the Services Subcontractor, especially the meetings recommended in Section 7.2.1. As a result services integration has improved.

(b) Word processing

Word processing is the facility by which standard letters, pro-formas, checklists, etc., can be stored on disk, entered into the computer and modified to suit individual circumstances. The relevant letter, report or checklist can then be produced by the computer and used as required by management. There are many instances indentified in Section 7.2 where such a facility would be useful, e.g. pre-tender reports, site reports, building regulation checklists.

(c) Information retrieval packages

The ability of the computer to act as a very efficient filing system is of particular use in recording the receipt of drawings, architects instructions, weather conditions, etc., (see Section 7.2.2). A wide range of standard packages are available to do this.

Take, for example, the receipt of drawings. The manager can, on the receipt of a drawing, enter the drawing number, revision number, date received, the trades to which it is relevant, the section of work to which it is related and any other criteria felt to be relevant. This information will then be stored on disk.

Subsequently, the information can be searched on the basis of any set of criteria specified by the manager. For instance, he can request all the drawings relevant to the Electrical Services Subcontractors for a particular section of the contract and the computer will provide him with a list of appropriate drawings.

This type of package has been found to be useful on projects where there are many services drawings that require cross-referencing with architectural drawings.

7.4.2 Possible future applications

Computer technology is developing at such a rapid rate that it is difficult to predict future trends. However, there are two areas in which computer assistance is possible that are well within the realms of possibility. They are:

(a) A project database
(b) Computer-aided draughting.

(a) A project database

A database is slightly more sophisticated than the information retrieval packages described in Section 7.4.1 in that it is a bank of data to which different people will want access to meet their own specific needs.

The Building Services Research and Information Association has conducted extensive research in this field [4] and has identified a system which, when the technology is available, could be used to assist services integration throughout the entire project.

The system would operate on a network of compatible computers, terminals and peripherals linked by data-transmission lines between the Architect, Services Consultant, Main Contractor and Services Subcontractor. At the commencement of the project, the Architect would open up computer files for all aspects of the project including the services installation. These files would be updated and used throughout the life of the project by the Services Consultant, Main Contractor and Services Subcontractor as follows:

(i) At the outline design stage, various combinations of environmental conditions with different building structures and fabrics, to ensure maximum comfort and minimum cost in use will be investigated.

(ii) At the detail design stage, once the best functional design has been achieved, a computer will be employed to check for clashes between services and the building fabric. These drawings would be in sufficient detail to serve as installation drawings. Programs with cost data would also automatically price these drawings.

(iii) At the installation stage the data base would then be used for ordering materials, planning, etc. Any variation orders would be fed into the system and would automatically update all the programmes, schedules and budgets. Feedback of progress information and installation details would also automatically update programmes and produce 'as-fitted' drawings.

(iv) Commissioning and maintenance manuals could also be produced from the database.

Such a system, although feasible, would also require the other recommendations in this chapter to be implemented, particularly those relating to managerial style.

(b) Computer-aided draughting

There are at present several computer-aided design packages on the market. Unfortunately, they are so large and expensive that they are only commercially viable for very large organizations requiring a high turnover of drawings. However, recent trends in computer technology indicate that it will only be a matter of time before the price and size is reduced.

The equipment (Fig. 7.1) necessary for a computer-aided draughting system is:

(i) Computer with a memory size of 256–512 kB

(ii) Disk or tape storage for all the information required to produce the drawings

(iii) Graphics terminal capable of producing high-resolution drawings

(iv) Digitizing board to enable information to be entered into the computer graphically

(v) Plotter to produce the final drawings.

Fig. 7.1 A typical microcomputer with digitizing tablet and printer

Using this equipment, a typical computer-aided draughting system will enable the user to:

(i) Determine whether or not two components are attempting to occupy the same space
(ii) Automatically measure dimensions between specified points
(iii) Move areas or shapes about the screen
(iv) Hatch different materials or types of equipment
(v) Superimpose one drawing on top of another
(vi) Rotate selected parts of the drawing through a specified angle
(vii) Enlarge certain parts of the drawing for clearer examination.

In addition the package will have a standard library of symbols, which the user will be able to place at specific locations on the screen.

Such a system will obviously be advantageous in assessing alternative solutions and should prevent many of the information co-ordination problems discussed in Section 7.2.2.

7.5 Guidelines for successful integration

It should be obvious by now that services integration is both complex and a major source of problems on the majority of building projects. Similarly, it should be obvious that there is no easy solution. However, it is possible to establish certain guidelines which, if followed, will assist in achieving successful integration. These guidelines can be summarized as follows:

(a) Create a matrix organization structure which incorporates the appropriate formal communication channels required by the JCT Contract yet encourages a network of communications within the project team.
(b) Produce long- and short-term production programmes based on network planning preferably with the aid of a site-based microcomputer.
(c) Maintain appropriate records and store on a site-based microcomputer for ease of retrieval as required.
(d) Complement these techniques and procedures by regular meetings between the Main Contractor and the Services Subcontractor.
(e) Adopt a democratic style of leadership and attempt to obtain the commitment of the Services Subcontractors to the goals of the project. Similarly, take advantage of any informal communications that arise on a project.
(f) Take advantage of future computer applications particularly in relation to a project database and computer-aided draughting, as and when they become smaller and cheaper.

Building Services Integration

References

(1) Butler, H., *Space requirements for building services distribution systems – detail design stage*, Technical Note TN3/79, Building Services Research and Information Association.

(2) Michie, A. and Ogle, J., *Co-ordination of building services – design stage methods*, Technical Note TN1/82, Building Services Research and Information Association.

(3) Michie, A. and Wix, J., *Co-ordination of Building Services – Computer-aided draughting*, Building Services Research and Information Association.

(4) Michie, A. and Ogle, J., *Co-ordination of building services – appraisal of influencing factors*, Building Services Research and Information Association.

Further reading

Bensasson, S., *Micros in construction*, Construction Industry Computing Association.

Index

131

Building Services Integration

Hot water pipework, 10
Human needs, 87
Human relations, 63, 82

IEE regulations, 57
Informal communications, 74, 90
Informal relations, 123
Information, 78, 81, 90–3, 117, 122
Information retrieval, 118, 125
Insulation, 12
Insurance, 118
Integrated suspended ceiling, 17
Interim certificate, 116–18
Intumescent material, 49
Intrinsic motivation, 87–9

JCT Standard Form of Contract, 110, 123, 128
Job satisfaction, 64

Leadership, 124, 128
Legitimate power, 79
Lift installations, 38, 42, 46, 53
Lighting, 11
Line and staff organization, 70–2
Location of services, 13
Location of plant, 14

Management, 76–93
Management structure, 64
Managers and their jobs, 76–7
Manager and power, 79–82
Manager and production, 77–9
Managerial skills, 82–4
Meetings, 109, 121, 128
Method statement, 98
Microcomputers, 124, 128
Mineral wool, 51
Monthly plan, 100
Motivation, 124

Network analysis, 102, 121, 125
Noise, 13
Nominated Subcontractor, 6, 98–9

Objectives, 65–6
Organic management, 85
Organizations, 62, 120
Organization structure, 70, 120

Payment, 124

Personal power, 80
Physical power, 81
Pipework, 12
Plant and equipment, 40
Precedence diagrams, 104, 121
Pre-contract planning, 99
Pre-tender planning, 99
Prime cost sum, 111
Production information, 97
Production planning, 77, 121
Profit, 65–6
Programme, 118, 122
Project data base, 126–28
Project information, 96
Project management, 120
Project organization, 62–75
Project performance, 66
Protected shaft, 46

Raised floors, 19
Reference information, 97
Refuse chutes, 11
Resource power, 79

Scaffold, 111, 113
Scientific management, 76
Services Consultant, 4, 110, 122, 127
Services Contractor, 79
Service core, 15, 38
Service hole, 58
Service outlet box, 25, 28
Service pipes, 110, 112
Service runs, 10, 14
Short term plan, 100, 128
Site diary, 118
Site information, 96
Site layout, 98
Site manager, 76, 80, 88
Skills of the manager, 82–4
Skirting trunking, 31
Social skills, 82
Sound insulation, 13, 56
Space allowances, 122
Span of control, 63
Specialist information, 96
Stage plan, 100
Strategic decisions, 78
Structural damage, 13
Structural floor, 12, 19, 43
Structural support, 42
Support systems, 34

132